THE WAY
PEOPLE
LIVE

Life in the North
During the Civil War
the
Civil War

Titles in The Way People Live series include:

Cowboys in the Old West
Life During the French Revolution
Life in Ancient Greece
Life in Ancient Rome
Life in an Eskimo Village
Life in the Elizabethan Theater
Life in the North During the Civil War
Life in the South During the Civil War
Life in the Warsaw Ghetto
Life in War-Torn Bosnia
Life on a Medieval Pilgrimage
Life on an Israeli Kibbutz

THE WAY PEOPLE LIVE

Life in the North During the Civil War

by Timothy Levi Biel

Lucent Books, P.O. Box 289011, San Diego, CA 92198-9011

Library of Congress Cataloging-in-Publication Data

Biel, Timothy L.
  Life in the North During the Civil War / by Timothy Levi Biel.
      p.   cm. — (The way people live)
  Includes bibliographical references and index.
  Summary: Describes urban, rural, and Union army camp life in the north-
ern United States during the bloodiest war in America's history.
  ISBN 1-56006-334-3 (alk. paper)
  1. United States—History—Civil War, 1861–1865—Social aspects—
Juvenile literature.   2. United States—Social conditions—To 1865—
Juvenile literature. [1. United States—History—Civil War, 1861–1865—
Social aspects.] I. Title. II. Series.
E468.9.B54   1997
973.7'1—dc20
                                                              96-34422
                                                              CIP
                                                              AC

Copyright 1997 by Lucent Books, Inc., P.O. Box 289011, San Diego, California
92198-9011

Printed in the U.S.A.

Contents

Discovering the Humanity in Us All

The Way People Live series focuses on pockets of human culture. Some of these are current cultures, like the Eskimos of the Arctic; others no longer exist, such as the Jewish ghetto in Warsaw during World War II. What many of these cultural pockets share, however, is the fact that they have been viewed before, but not completely understood.

To really understand any culture, it is necessary to strip the mind of the common notions we hold about groups of people. These stereotypes are the archenemies of learning. It does not even matter whether the stereotypes are positive or negative; they are confining and tight. Removing them is a challenge that's not easily met, as anyone who has ever tried it will admit. Ideas that do not fit into the templates we create are unwelcome visitors—ones we would prefer remain quietly in a corner or forgotten room.

The cowboy of the Old West is a good example of such confining roles. The cowboy was courageous, yet soft-spoken. His time (it is always a he, in our template) was spent alternatively saving a rancher's daughter from certain death on a runaway stagecoach, or shooting it out with rustlers. At times, of course, he was likely to get a little crazy in town after a trail drive, but for the most part, he was the epitome of inner strength. It is disconcerting to find out that the cowboy is human, even a bit childish. Can it really be true that cowboys would line up to help the cook on the trail drive grind coffee, just hoping he would give them a little stick of pep-permint candy that came with the coffee shipment? The idea of tough cowboys vying with one another to help "Coosie" (as they called their cooks) for a bit of candy seems silly and out of place.

So is the vision of Eskimos playing video games and watching MTV, living in prefab housing in the Arctic. It just does not fit with what "Eskimo" means. We are far more comfortable with snow igloos and whale blubber, harpoons and kayaks.

Although the cultures dealt with in Lucent's The Way People Live series are often historically and socially well known, the emphasis is on the personal aspects of life. Groups of people, while unquestionably affected by their politics and their governmental structures, are more than those institutions. How do people in a particular time and place educate their children? What do they eat? And how do they build their houses? What kinds of work do they do? What kinds of games do they enjoy? The answers to these questions bring these cultures to life. People's lives are revealed in the particulars and only by knowing the particulars can we understand these cultures' will to survive and their moments of weakness and greatness.

This is not to say that understanding politics does not help to understand a culture. There is no question that the Warsaw ghetto, for example, was a culture that was brought about by the politics and social ideas of Adolf Hitler and the Third Reich. But the Jews who were crowded together in the ghetto cannot be understood by the Reich's politics. Their life was a day-to-day battle for existence, and the creativity and methods they used to prolong their lives is a vital story of human perseverance that would be denied by focusing only on the institutions of Hitler's Germany. Knowing that children as young as five or six outwitted Nazi guards on a daily basis, that Jewish policemen helped the Germans control the ghetto, that children attended secret schools in the ghetto and even earned diplomas—these are the things that reveal the fabric of life, that can inspire, intrigue, and amaze.

Books in the The Way People Live series allow both the casual reader and the student to see humans as victims, heroes, and onlookers. And although humans act in ways that can fill us with feelings of sorrow and revulsion, it is important to remember that "hero," "predator," and "victim" are dangerous terms. Heaping undue pity or praise on people reduces them to objects, and strips them of their humanity.

Seeing the Jews of Warsaw only as victims is to deny their humanity. Seeing them only as they appear in surviving photos, staring at the camera with infinite sadness, is limiting, both to them and to those who want to understand them. To an object of pity, the only appropriate response becomes "Those poor creatures!" and that reduces both the quality of their struggle and the depth of their despair. No one is served by such two-dimensional views of people and their cultures.

With this in mind, the The Way People Live series strives to flesh out the traditional, two-dimensional views of people in various cultures and historical circumstances. Using a wide variety of primary quotations—the words not only of the politicians and government leaders, but of the real people whose lives are being examined—each book in the series attempts to show an honest and complete picture of a culture removed from our own by time or space.

By examining cultures in this way, the reader will notice not only the glaring differences from his or her own culture, but also will be struck by the similarities. For indeed, people share common needs—warmth, good company, stability, and affirmation from others. Ultimately, seeing how people really live, or have lived can only enrich our understanding of ourselves.

Civil War: A Tragic Chapter in American Life

On the evening of April 11, 1861, George T. Strong, a successful, forty-one-year-old lawyer from New York City, attended a dinner at the elegant estate of John Astor, the governor of New York and one of the wealthiest men in America. According to Strong's personal diary, which has been preserved to this day, many of the state's most powerful legislators, judges, and businessmen were at Astor's home that night.

Within the main wing of the red brick mansion, built in the old Federalist style, Strong and the other guests were greeted by a butler who took their hats and coats before ushering them into the front parlor. Beneath the wide span of a chandelier bearing a hundred or more little gaslights in the shape of candles, the reflections of ladies in long dresses with wide, hooped crinoline skirts, and men in their long black coats could be seen in a huge, gold-framed mirror on one wall of the parlor. It made the room, which was large enough to hold forty people comfortably, look twice its size. The walls of the brightly lit room with its long, stately windows and velvet curtains were lined with Louis XIV–style chairs and love seats with embroidered cushions and intricately carved cherry-wood arms and legs.

In the parlor, Strong and the other male guests mingled and talked. On this night, the topic on almost everyone's mind was the showdown between President Abraham Lincoln and Jefferson Davis, the president of the

When Abraham Lincoln was inaugurated on March 4, 1861, seven Southern states had already seceded from the Union and formed a new nation, known as the Confederate States of America.

new Southern Confederacy. In November 1860, Lincoln, a vocal opponent of slavery, had been elected the sixteenth president of the United States. Many Southerners interpreted Lincoln's election as the final insult from Northerners after decades of bitter disagreements and half-hearted compromises over the issue of slavery. Knowing that Lincoln and the Republicans wanted to outlaw slavery in all new U.S. states and territories, most Southern slave owners feared that Lincoln's election was a first step toward abolishing slavery in their states as well. These slave owners, who were the wealthiest and most powerful men in the South, were so angry over Lincoln's election that by the time of his inauguration, on March 4, 1861, the states of South Carolina, Mississippi, Florida, Alabama, Georgia, Louisiana, and Texas had already decided to secede from the United States of America.

In February 1861, delegates from these seven states voted to form a new nation, the Confederate States of America. After adopting a constitution almost identical to that of the United States—but specifically preserving the rights of states to permit and regulate slavery—the Confederate delegates elected Jefferson Davis, a former U.S. senator from Mississippi, as their nation's first president. Shortly after his inauguration, Davis declared that all U.S. Army personnel located in the Confederate States represented a foreign power, and he demanded that they withdraw.

President Lincoln believed that the Constitution did not permit a state to withdraw from the Union. Therefore, he refused to recognize the Confederacy as a legitimate nation and refused to withdraw the eighty-six-man force occupying Fort Sumter, South Carolina. This tiny fort in Charleston Harbor along the Atlantic coast was one of the few places in the South where U.S. soldiers were

Jefferson Davis, the popular U.S. senator from Mississippi, was elected president of the Southern Confederacy.

stationed. Most Northerners doubted that this upstart nation, without a standing army, would actually challenge U.S. troops.

But they underestimated the Southerners' resolve. By April 9, Jefferson Davis had managed to assemble an army of six thousand men in Charleston. Then he demanded the surrender of Major Robert Anderson, the U.S. commander at Fort Sumter.

At dinner tables and evening gatherings around the country, Northerners and Southerners alike speculated about the outcome of this cat-and-mouse game between Lincoln and Davis. At the Astor party in New York, most of the guests agreed with George Strong that the Confederates were bluffing and would not risk war with the Union, which was much bigger, and richer.

The following night, April 12, 1861, Strong was shocked to discover the Confederates' boldness. After attending a meeting in downtown New York with fellow members of Trinity Church, Strong accompanied two friends for a stroll uptown. When they reached Fifth Avenue, they heard newsboys hawking special editions of the *New York Tribune* and *New York Herald*.

"Extry! Extry!" the newsboys barked. "Confederates bombard Fort Sumter!" At first, Strong did not believe it. He and his friends concluded that "it was probably a sell and we would not be sold." They continued to walk "about four more blocks," when they heard more newsboys shouting the same headline.

"We could stand it no longer," Strong wrote. "I sacrificed six pence and read the news by the light of a corner gas lamp." The next day, Saturday, April 13, 1861, he wrote in his diary, "April 13. Here begins a new chapter of my journal entitled WAR."[1]

The new chapter in George Strong's diary turned out to be longer and more tragic than he—or anyone else—expected. At age forty-one, Strong was a little old to volunteer for active duty, but his diary reflects all the fervor, anguish, euphoria, and relief that the men, women, and children on the home front

After demanding the withdrawal of U.S. troops from Fort Sumter in South Carolina, Jefferson Davis and his Confederates bombarded the fortress, reducing it to ruins.

experienced during the four long years of America's bloodiest and costliest war. More than a century later, the words of people like George Strong offer us a candid view of what life was like in the Northern United States during the Civil War.

These people lived through the bloodiest war in America's history. Over 620,000 Americans were killed in the Civil War. Twice that many were wounded, and another million were imprisoned. Such widespread disaster affected virtually every person living in America. And yet, since most of the actual fighting took place in the South, the effects in the North were often subtle or indirect. Many children, for example, stayed home from school and worked on farms and in factories, especially if their fathers had joined the army. More than half the Northern population still lived on farms, where mothers and children often worked in the fields all day after rising at dawn to do chores around the house. In city factories as well, working-class women and children filled the gaps left by men who had gone to war. This book explores what it must have been like to live during this unsettled time, perhaps the most turbulent period in our nation's history.

The Wheels of Change

Since the framing of the Constitution, the essential political difference between Northern and Southern states was the legality of slavery. Almost every political confrontation between Northern and Southern states was somehow tied to this issue. As the nation grew and added new states, the slavery issue became more complex and entangled. After seventy-five years of leapfrogging from one weak compromise to another, in 1861, with Abraham Lincoln installed as the sixteenth president of the United States, both sides had run out of compromises.

Still, it would be misleading to claim that Northerners went to war to help slaves gain their freedom. While a tiny minority of Northern abolitionists wanted to end slavery in the Southern states on the grounds that it was immoral, the vast majority of Northerners just wanted to keep slavery from spreading. Their reasons usually had more to do with economic security than with moral issues or with the plight of the Negro slaves. The economic differences between North and South had been widening ever since the U.S. Constitution had become effective in 1789. But by 1860, dramatic economic

The controversial issue of slavery pitted Northerners against Southerners. Although most Northerners did not want slavery to spread to new states, their reasons were based on economics rather than morality.

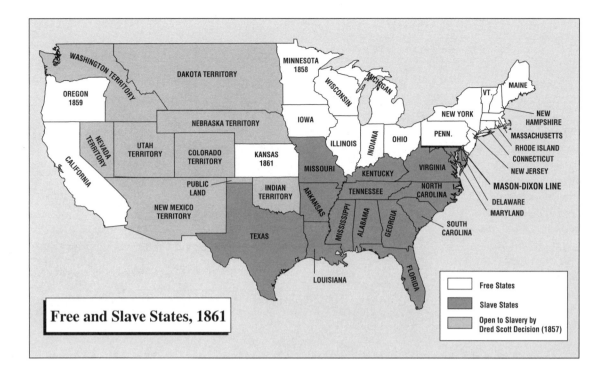

Free and Slave States, 1861

Legend:
- Free States
- Slave States
- Open to Slavery by Dred Scott Decision (1857)

changes, especially in the North, had driven an enormous wedge between the two regions. Attitudes toward slavery in both North and South reflected these ever-widening differences.

A Time of Growth and Promise

The population of the entire United States was growing rapidly. In fact, between 1840 and 1860, the American population nearly doubled, from 17 million to 32 million. Some of this growth came from the addition of Texas in 1845 and other cessions from Mexico in 1846, California in 1850, and Oregon in 1859. The addition of these western states practically doubled the physical size of the United States, but were sparsely populated compared to the Northeast, where the greatest population growth occurred, as a result of massive immigration from Europe. Waves of immigrants settled in the Northern cities because the newcomers had heard of the great need for labor there. By 1860, 4 million foreign-born immigrants lived in the United States, and two-thirds of them had arrived between 1850 and 1860!

On the Move!

One of the most conspicuous signs of the rapid growth and change in the North was the spread of railroad lines. This may explain why poet Walt Whitman and so many other American writers of the nineteenth century used the image of the steam locomotive to symbolize the effects of industrialization. Between 1840 and 1860, the amount of railroad track in the United States jumped from thirty-three hundred miles to thirty-one thousand miles. This exceeded the miles of

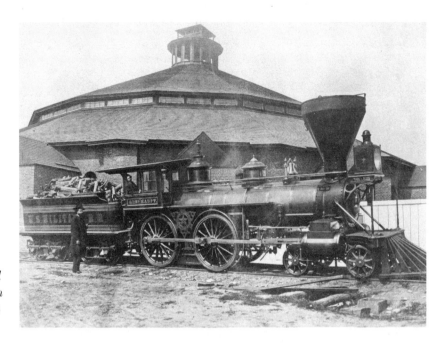

Between 1840 and 1860, the railroad in the United States expanded greatly—from thirty-three hundred miles of track to an incredible thirty-one thousand miles. This expansion helped industrialize the United States and the Northern manufacturing states in particular.

railroad track in the rest of the world combined! Most of these railroad tracks covered the Northern manufacturing states—Massachusetts, Rhode Island, New York, New Jersey, Pennsylvania, and Ohio. Trains brought raw materials—cotton from the South, wool and iron ore from the Midwest—to factories in northeastern cities, where shoes and clothing, farm tools and machines, and, of course, more railroad tracks and cars were manufactured.

America's great network of canals and waterways also contributed to the new, industrial North. The river steamboat had been invented by American Robert Fulton in 1807. "The dozen or so steamboats on American rivers in 1815," says James McPherson, "multiplied to about three thousand by 1860."[2] Contributing to this growing river commerce was an expansion of America's system of canals. Like the new railroad lines, most of these canals were built in the North, and they ran in an east-west direction.

The Weakening Ties Between North and South

The new railroads and canal routes signified an important effect of the industrial revolution. Regional loyalties and business ties were changing. Before 1840, most railroad and steamboat lines ran north and south, connecting the producers of cotton, rice, and meat in the South with buyers and manufacturers in the North. These routes followed the Atlantic seaboard and the routes of the Ohio and Mississippi Rivers. But the great majority of new canals and railroads built between 1840 and 1860 ran east and west, connecting the Northeast with Ohio, Michigan, Indiana, and Illinois. By the 1850s, the freight shipped on east-west canals and railroad lines was more than twice that of the freight moving north and south.

These facts reveal that the east-west ties among Northern states were growing tighter, while the bonds between North and South

A Romantic's View of the Locomotive

Walt Whitman (1819–1892), the great American poet, became a field nurse during the Civil War, and his firsthand experience of its death and misery disturbed him deeply. Likewise, the assassination of Abraham Lincoln inspired him to compose "O Captain, My Captain," one of the most moving poems ever written. Neither of these events, however, could shake Whitman's resolute faith in the spirit and energy of America, which he celebrated in a number of his works. The poem that follows, taken from Literature: An Introduction to Poetry, Prose, and Drama, *edited by X. J. Kennedy, reflects a common nineteenth-century theme: the locomotive as a symbol of modern technology. Whitman romanticized this technology as an expression of the industry, the innovation, the independence, the strength, and the robust spirit of America.*

To a Locomotive in Winter

Thee for my recitative,
Thee in the driving storm even as now, the
   snow, the winter-day declining,

Thee in thy panoply, thy measur'd dual throb-
   bing and thy beat convulsive,
Thy black cylindric body, golden brass and sil-
   very steel,
Thy ponderous side-bars, parallel and connecting rods, gyrating, shuttling at thy sides,
Thy metrical, now swelling pant and roar, now
   tapering in the distance,
Thy great protruding head-light fix'd in front,
Thy long, pale, floating vapor-pennants,
   tinged with delicate purple,
The dense and murky clouds out-belching
   from thy smoke-stack,
Thy knitted frame, thy springs and valves, the
   tremulous twinkle of thy wheels,
The train of cars behind, obedient, merrily
   following,
Through gale or calm, now swift, now slack,
   yet steadily careering;
Type of the modern—emblem of motion and
   power—pulse of the continent,
For once come serve the Muse and merge in
   verse, even as here I see thee,
With storm and buffeting gusts of wind and
   falling snow,
By day thy warning ringing bell to sound its
   notes,
By night thy silent signal lamps to swing.
Fierce-throated beauty!
Roll through my chant with all thy lawless
   music, thy swinging lamps at night,
Thy madly-whistled laughter, echoing, rum-
   bling like an earthquake, rousing all,
Law of thyself complete, thine own track
   firmly holding,
(No sweetness debonair of tearful harp or glib
   piano thine,)
Thy trills of shrieks by rocks and hills return'd,
Launch'd o'er the prairies wide, across the
   lakes,
To the free skies unpent and glad and strong.

Walt Whitman

Edward Dicey, an English journalist, wrote about his 1862 travels through the United States. As quoted in George Winston Smith and Charles Judah's Life in the North During the Civil War, *Dicey describes Americans as "a travelling people." This was true; especially since the advent of steam-powered travel by rail or by boat, millions of Americans seemed constantly "on the move."*

"When the war commenced, many feared the destruction of railroads in the North, and the interruption of trade and travel from rebel raids; but these were few and far between. The increase of travel became so great that companies could scarcely furnish carriages to convey passengers and the numerous troops hastening to the fields of conflict in the South. Whole families, even of the poorest of people, travelled extensively; in fact the Americans are a travelling people, few living where they were born; and most travel in search of better locations, so that railroads and steamboats are often crowded, and the vast prairies often dotted by the white tents and moving wagons of thousands of emigrants, going farther west with their numerous herds, in search of richer lands, larger farms, and better homes."

Emigrants from the East journey across the prairies. During the Civil War era, many Americans packed up their belongings and headed west.

were loosening. As the industrial revolution brought change to the North far more rapidly than to the South, the differences between these two regions became magnified. The differences were most obvious, of course, with respect to policies concerning slavery, but they were entwined with several others that increasingly isolated the Southern states.

In the South, most of the wealth and political clout remained in the hands of slave owners. Their huge rice, tobacco, sugar, and cotton plantations dwarfed the typical Northern farm, which was usually just large enough to support the owner and his family. Both the economy and the culture of the South discouraged rapid changes of the kind that occurred in the North. The Southern image of prosperity was personified by the cultured gentleman farmer. Black slaves and white slave handlers worked and managed the land, while the plantation owner rode his fine horses to the county seat or state capital to see to the region's political affairs. Labor, at least in its traditional form, was beneath him.

In the North, the *image* of the laborer enjoyed greater respect. While unskilled factory workers were paid pitifully low wages and made to live and work in conditions that were not much better than those of some Southern slaves, most Northerners managed to overlook this reality. Beyond it they envisioned the American dream: if a man worked hard enough and smart enough, he could escape poverty and rise to the highest levels of wealth and success. Hard work and intelligence were the keys.

"A Land of Opportunity"— For Some

For many Northerners, the West was the ultimate symbol of this "equal opportunity." That is what prompted newspaper publisher Horace Greeley's famous recommendation: "Go West, young man!" According to Greeley, "The public lands are the great regulator of the relations of Labor and Capital, the safety valve of our industrial and social engine."[3] Theoretically, even men, women, and children who earned less than a dollar for working a fifteen- or sixteen-hour day in a sweatshop or freezing cold factory could always pack up and move west to seek their fortune.

Factory workers in the North were subjected to low wages and poor living and working conditions, much like the oppressed slaves in the South.

Most Northerners Welcome Progress

Willingness to not only accept but welcome change dramatically altered life in the North. It also helped to tear the North and South apart. In the North, change was valued above tradition. Over and over, politicians and reformers used words like "progress," "advancement," and "improvement." An editorialist for the *New York Times* exulted in the 1840s, "Custom hath lost its sway, and Time and Change are the Champions against the field."[4] Most Northerners welcomed the changes of the industrial revolution. One enthusiast characterized railroads as "God's instrument to quicken the activity of men; to send energy and vitality where before were silence and barrenness; to multiply cities and villages, studded with churches, dotted with schools."[5] In 1851, a writer for *Scientific*

American asserted that "every new and useful machine, invented and improved, confers a general benefit upon all classes—the poor as well as the rich."[6] Northerners' acceptance of new innovations helped them increase their production until, by 1860, the United States was second in the world to England in manufacturing. Four out of every five dollars of this new wealth were made by people living in the North.

New England: Birthplace of Free Public Education

Along with their acceptance of technological change, most Northerners recognized the importance of educating all children and young people, not just those whose parents could pay for their schooling. In fact, the idea of free public education for all citizens was

Resistance to Change

Thanks to the steam engine and other inventions, machines began to take over some of the work that had been done by men. Although the number of jobs created by this process eventually exceeded the number of jobs it eliminated, the men who were forced to change jobs often resisted. On July 9, 1862, the New York Times *reported the futile efforts of dockworkers to halt the use of steam-powered grain elevators for loading grain onto steamships.*

"About two thousand men have been employed in this city, in handling the immense quantity of grain that arrives here from the West. These men are called 'strikers,' 'shovelers,' and 'trimmers.' Dur-

ing the last season, there were introduced into the harbor two 'grain elevators,' which readily performed the work of many men, and did it much more rapidly. This season, five more elevators have appeared, so that altogether the machines in use will perform about two-thirds the work required. The men have heretofore formed a Protective Union, and have resolved not to work in connection with the elevators, or for any man who employs them. They contend that the great dust which the elevators raise is injurious to life, and furthermore that the manner in which the ships are loaded often causes the cargoes to shift, the ships to roll and ultimately to sink and be lost."

Schools in New England offered free public education to all children and young people, giving both the rich and the poor the opportunity to better themselves.

born in New England. European countries did not begin to offer it until late in the nineteenth century. Wealthy Europeans, like the wealthy class of the American South, recognized that public education could weaken their political and financial control. As one Southern plantation owner put it, "Is this the way to produce producers? To make every child in the state a literary character would not be a good qualification for those who must live by manual labor."[7]

Indeed, many technological innovations were invented by members of the working class. Elias Howe, for example, was a machinist in a Boston factory when he invented the sewing machine in the 1840s. Many other manual laborers made important improvements to manufacturing methods. This "Yankee ingenuity" did not go unnoticed by European competitors. A visiting British industrialist reported in 1854 that even the lower-class schoolboy in America

> was educated up to a far higher standard than those of a much superior social level in the Old World. The American working boy develops rapidly into the skilled

artisan, and having once mastered one part of his business, he is never content until he has mastered all. . . . [With examples] constantly before him of ingenious men who have solved economic and mechanical problems to their own profit and elevation . . . there is not a working boy of average ability in the New England States, at least, who has not an idea of some mechanical invention or improvement in manufactures.[8]

While this description of the average American schoolboy clearly exaggerates the technical expertise of the country's youth, it shows the ideal that most Northern educators envisioned. Increasingly, wealth in the North was accumulated by manufacturers, business owners, bankers, and inventors. Millionaires and wealthy families cropped up in growing numbers in Northern cities. At a time when a family could live comfortably on $5,000 per year, New York City boasted more than eight hundred families with incomes over $100,000 per year.

As early as 1830, Massachusetts and New York had public school systems. In 1839

Education pioneer Horace Mann (pictured) established the first teacher-training school in the United States. His "normal school" was soon adopted across the nation.

Horace Mann, the secretary of the Massachusetts State Board of Education, founded the first school for teacher training, called a "normal school" because it stressed the standards or "normal expectations" for students at various grade levels. Soon many states established their own normal schools following the Massachusetts model. Massachusetts also became a leader in establishing mandatory attendance laws, and in 1852, it became the first state to offer a free, public high school education to any citizen of the state. By 1860, most Northern states had public school systems through at least the eighth grade, and about three-quarters of all Northern children between five and sixteen years of age were enrolled in school.

Horace Mann believed that education would give the poor the tools they needed to escape from poverty: "Education does better than to disarm the poor of their hostility toward the rich; it prevents their being poor." He summarized the North's modern vision of education as an agent for social and economic change:

> Education is the grand agent for the development . . . of national resources, more powerful in the production and gainful employment of the total wealth of a country than all the other things mentioned in the books of the political economists.[9]

Rising Literacy Rates

With broader education came a larger reading public and more newspapers. By 1860, the United States had twice as many newspapers as Britain. In fact, it had nearly one-third of the newspapers in the entire world, and nearly 80 percent of these were published in Northern cities and towns.

Rising literacy rates also contributed to advances in technology. The first steam-powered printing press began operation in 1835, increasing printing capacity from 200 copies per hour to over 5,000 copies per hour. The invention of the telegraph in 1844 made possible the instantaneous reporting of news over long distances. This, in turn, led to the formation of the Associated Press in 1848. In addition, the expansion of railroads enabled city newspapers to print weekly editions and distribute them in rural areas. Including its rural distribution, Horace Greeley's *New York Tribune* reached a circulation of 200,000 copies by 1850.

The Work Ethic

Underlying the push for literacy and education in the North was the Protestant Calvinist doctrine sometimes known as the Puritan ethic. According to this doctrine, work glorifies

God and idleness is the instrument of Satan. Calvinist preachers often quoted biblical passages that emphasized the importance of work, such as 2 Thessalonians 3:10: "If any would not work, neither shall he eat." Proverbs 13:11 was another passage popular with the Calvinist preachers: "Wealth gotten by vanity shall be diminished; but he that gathereth by labour shall increase." Remnants of this doctrine remain with us to this day in such familiar sayings as "idle hands do devil's work."

The work ethic permeated the public schools of the nineteenth century, both directly and indirectly. School readers reminded children that "industry is a SOLEMN DUTY you owe to God, whose command is 'BE DILIGENT IN BUSINESS!'" The famous *McGuffey Reader*, which was used in American public schools as late as the 1930s, advised that "persevering industry [hard work over the long term] will enable one to accomplish almost anything."[10]

Religious overtones in the public schools of the nineteenth century were obvious. The Massachusetts superintendent of schools in 1857 wrote that an essential task of education was "by moral and religious instruction daily given to inculcate [impress upon students] habits of regularity, punctuality, constancy, and industry."[11] Because it encouraged the same values that bosses looked for in workers, the Protestant work ethic contributed to the modernization of the North.

The Other Side of the Coin: The Working Class

While modernization brought thousands of new jobs to the North, it hardly made workers rich. In fact, the surplus of cheap immigrant labor enabled business owners to offer wages that were barely enough to live on. As a larger share of the Northern population

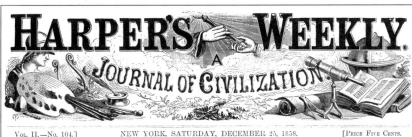

Rising literacy rates were responsible for the success of newspapers like Harper's Weekly. *By 1860, the United States produced nearly one-third of all newspapers in the world.*

went to work for others, the working-class share of the wealth actually declined. At the time of the Civil War, approximately 30 percent of all Americans held 90 percent of all the money made in America. Wealth was becoming increasingly concentrated in the hands of a few.

The widening gap between rich and poor seemed to indicate that something was amiss in the North. The Republicans continued to preach the work ethic and the principle of equal opportunity. Party spokesman Henry Carey claimed that "the interests of the capitalist and the laborer are in perfect harmony with each other,"[12] but many others were not so sure. By the end of the 1850s, the North was gripped by a restlessness, a sense that something was not working.

A Growing Restlessness

As modernization progressed in the North, so did the restlessness of the people. Ironically, the values that fostered modernization were now being threatened by its results. The Protestant ethic taught self-improvement through self-discipline, industry, thrift, and sobriety. But along with the modern factories and growing cities came poverty, overcrowding, crime, drunkenness, and prostitution. Many intellectuals and reformers were concerned that the changes brought on by industrialization had happened too fast. Rather than being in control of this new technology, some Northerners felt that it was controlling them. The industrial revolution was like a runaway locomotive, and the people on board were just hanging on for the ride. "We do not ride on the railroad," said Henry David Thoreau. "It rides on us."[13]

The immigrants composed one group of Northerners who often felt that the runaway locomotive of industrialization was running right over them. Many Europeans who came to America after 1840 were from Ireland and Germany, and a majority of them were Roman Catholic. Many of them did not speak English, and often they did not send their children to the public schools. Since the newly arrived Europeans also made up a large portion of the working poor, a natural tension arose between them and the middle- and upper-class businessmen, who were predominantly Protestant.

Members of the growing class of industrial workers were frustrated and angry over the discrepancy between the ideals of the work ethic and the realities of the workplace. While they witnessed many wealthy individuals benefiting directly from modernization, they did not always share the Republicans' optimism that "reform" or "progress" benefited society as a whole. Roman Catholic doctrine reinforced this antiprogressive view. In 1859 a prominent Catholic layman wrote, "The age attaches too much importance to what is called the progress of society or the progress of civilization, which, to the man whose eye is fixed on God and eternity, can appear of not great value."[14]

Protestant reformers countered that the poverty of the working class resulted from the sin of laziness. They pointed out that only about one-third of the immigrant families sent their children to the public schools. Immigrants responded that many poor children had to work to help support their families. Therefore the families could not even afford the luxury of accepting a free education. Some immigrants also suspected that the public schools brainwashed their children, forcing them to forget the traditions and abandon the language of their own people.

A Northern gentleman helps newly arrived immigrants find their way in a new city. Many European immigrants became part of the North's working poor and found life in the United States an endless struggle.

Equal Opportunity: More Than a Slogan?

As tensions mounted in the North, many Americans, especially Southerners, believed that Northerners should have been less concerned about slavery and more concerned about inequities in their own region. They pointed out that Northerners were quick to criticize the mistreatment of slaves in the South, while in Northern cities, workers were being treated almost as badly as slaves. George Fitzhugh, a Southern writer and social philosopher, taunted Northerners, accusing them of hypocrisy:

> Equality, where are thy monuments? Deep, deep in the bowels of the earth, where women and children drag out their lives in darkness harnessed like horses to heavy cars loaded with ore. Or

in some grand, gloomy and monotonous factory, where pallid children work fourteen hours a day and go home at night to sleep in damp cellars. It may be too that this cellar contains aged parents too old to work, and cast off by their employer to die. Great railroads and mighty steamships too, thou mayest boast, but still the operatives who construct them are beings destined to poverty and neglect. . . . The sordid spirit of mammon [material wealth] presides o'er all, and from all proceed the sighs and groans of the oppressed.[15]

Many Northerners also noted this irony. Even Abraham Lincoln bemoaned the age of corrupted values, saying, "We have grown fat . . . greedy to be masters."[16] Among the most insightful observers of the day were those who recognized that greed infected both

Harriet Beecher Stowe's controversial novel Uncle Tom's Cabin *not only condemned slavery but also criticized the exploitation of Northern workers.*

North and South. Harriet Beecher Stowe, whose novel *Uncle Tom's Cabin* stirred numerous Northerners to take up the abolitionist cause, attacked the inhumanity of slavery. Often overlooked, however, are Stowe's harsh criticisms of those who exploited workers in the North. The most evil villain in the book is Simon Legree, the transplanted Northerner who uses his plantation in the South "as he did everything else, merely as an implement for making money."[17] Meanwhile, the most heroic figure in the novel, Augustine St. Clare, reminds the reader that "the American planter is only doing, in another form, what the English aristocracy and capitalists are doing by the lower classes, that is, I take it, appropriating them, body and bone, soul and spirit, to their use and convenience."[18]

While the first half of the nineteenth century had been a period of great optimism in the North, that optimism was beginning to give way to a growing sense of concern in the 1850s and 1860s. Northerners feared that if the slavery issue were not resolved, their union with the South would not last. And at least some Northerners harbored a sense of guilt or shame because society had turned its back on the principles of equality.

Although Northerners had welcomed the industrial revolution with open arms, they had paid only lip service to the Republican ideal of equal opportunity for all. By 1861, they were forced to pay a much higher price.

A Call to Arms

At 7:00 P.M. on April 13, 1861, Major Robert Anderson, the commander of the tiny force of eighty-six Union soldiers who manned Fort Sumter, surrendered to the six-thousand-man Confederate army whose cannons had bombarded the fort from the shores of Charleston, South Carolina. Before that moment, Northerners were unsure how they felt about the South's secession. Most Northern abolitionists so despised the practice of slavery that they did not want anything to do with the South. "If South Carolina wants to leave," read one editorial in the *Chicago Tribune*, "let her go, and like a limb lopped from a healthy trunk, wilt and rot where she falls."[19] Horace Greeley expressed a similar opinion in his *New York Tribune*: "If the Cotton States shall become satisfied that they can do better out of the Union than in it, we insist on letting them go."[20] The abolitionists, however, made up only a small minority in the North.

True, the majority of Northerners opposed the spread of slavery, but most of them also supported the right of Southern states to decide the legality of slavery for themselves. In fact, there was widespread fear among Northerners, especially among the immigrants who held low-paying, unskilled manufacturing jobs, that abolishing slavery in the South would cause thousands of former slaves to converge on the North and take their jobs away from them. Most of these immigrants had voted against Lincoln in the election of November 1860, supporting the Northern Democrat Stephen Douglas, instead. The Douglas

THE "SECESSION MOVEMENT".

A Civil War–era cartoon derides Southern states for seceding from the Union. Prior to the bombing of Fort Sumter, many Northerners had believed the Union would be better off without the rebellious Southerners.

A Call to Arms **25**

Abraham Lincoln (at podium) and Stephen Douglas debate prior to the 1860 presidential election. Although both candidates worked toward a compromise on the slavery issue, Douglas won the support of immigrants who feared the abolishment of slavery would endanger their jobs.

instead. The Douglas Democrats made crude references to Lincoln and Northern abolitionists as "nigger lovers," and they tried to arouse immigrants in the North with hysterical threats. "If you want to support a party that says a nigger is better than an Irishman, vote for the Republican candidate,"[21] Douglas warned. Douglas was especially popular in border states like Kansas, Illinois, Indiana, Ohio, and West Virginia. Slavery was illegal in these states, but many residents counted slave owners among their friends and relatives, and hoped that a compromise could still be worked out between the two sides.

Though Douglas Democrats tried to portray Lincoln as a radical abolitionist, the Republican candidate also hoped for a compromise. Lincoln detested slavery, but he had campaigned on his willingness to come to an agreement with the slave states. He had proposed that slavery remain legal in the South as long as no new states or territories were permitted to adopt the practice. This containment of slavery, he believed, would lead to its gradual death.

Of course, that is exactly what Southern slave owners feared and why they had spearheaded the move to secede. As soon as Lincoln was inaugurated, Southern leaders acted swiftly and boldly, hoping to take advantage of the restlessness and disagreement in the North; but they overestimated the extent of the disagreement. Although Northerners could not agree on the issue of slavery, the threat of war and the prospect of dividing the nation in two brought Northerners together in a way that nothing else could have. News of Major Anderson's surrender flooded the Northern states by telegraph, newspaper, and word of mouth. Cries to let the South go, and even voices urging compromise, were drowned by patriotic fervor and calls to arms. Stephen Douglas went to the White House to assure President Lincoln of his support for a war to preserve the Union. "There can be no neutrals in this war," declared Douglas, "only patriots—or traitors!"[22] Now that war appeared imminent, the abolitionists embraced the idea of fighting to keep the South in the Union. The same *Chicago Tribune* editorialist who had so recently urged Lincoln to "let her go," now viewed the war as the fulfillment of the prophecy made by John Brown, the famous abolitionist martyr: "I hear Old John Brown knocking on the lid of his coffin and shouting 'let me out, let me out!' The doom of slavery is at hand. It is to be wiped out in blood!"[23]

Lincoln Reacts Cautiously to Southern Secession

While Northerners of every political stripe called for retaliation and war against the South, President Lincoln took a tactful, measured, and tolerant response. He believed that most Southerners opposed secession but had been forced to accept it by the powerful minority of slave owners. Just two weeks before the bombardment of Fort Sumter, Lincoln directed his first inaugural speech to these moderate Southerners. He pledged not "to interfere with the institution of slavery where it exists," and he closed the address with this impassioned appeal for reconciliation:

> We are not enemies, but friends. We must not be enemies. Though passion may have strained, it must not break our bonds of affection. The mystic chords of memory, stretching from every battlefield, and patriot grave, to every living heart and hearthstone, all over this broad land, will yet swell by the chorus

of the Union, when again touched, as surely they will be, by the better angels of our nature.[24]

War Fever Sweeps the North

Walking a political tightrope, Lincoln carefully avoided any mention of slavery. He knew that the majority of Northerners would not have been willing to fight a war against slavery, but they were practically demanding a war to overthrow the Confederate government and save the Union. If the Southern states were permitted to withdraw from the Union at will, the reasoning went, the federal government would be exposed as a powerless institution incapable of enforcing its own constitution. "We must fight now," declared an Indiana newspaper, "not because we want to subjugate the South . . . but because we *must!* The Nation has been defied. The National Government has been assailed. If either can be done with impunity . . . we are not a Nation, and our Government is a sham."[25] The *Chicago Journal* proclaimed that the South had "outraged the Constitution, set at defiance all law, and trampled under foot that flag which has been the glorious and consecrated symbol of American Liberty."[26] Democrats as well as Republicans declared their determination to save the Union. "We were born and bred under the stars and stripes," wrote a Pittsburgh Democrat. "When the South becomes an enemy to the American system of government . . . and fires upon the flag . . . our influence goes for that flag, no matter whether a Republican or a Democrat holds it."[27]

Most political, religious, and civic leaders in the North interpreted this war fever as a sign of moral courage. It showed that despite the division, jealousy, and materialism that had been sweeping the nation, most Northerners were still willing to face the prospect of war over a strongly held principle. Horace Greeley, editor of the *New York Tribune*, summarized this widespread feeling:

> Let no one feel that our present troubles are deplorable, in view of the majestic development of Nationality and Patriotism which they have occasioned. But yesterday we were esteemed a sordid, grasping, money-loving people, too greedy to gain to cherish generous and lofty aspirations. Today vindicates us from that reproach, and demonstrates that beneath the scum and slag of forty years of peace, and in spite of the insidious approaches of corruption the fires of patriotic devotion are still burning.[28]

Raising a Volunteer Army

As the call for war grew louder, President Lincoln took the first cautious steps to prepare for war. Citing "combinations too powerful to be suppressed by the ordinary course of judicial proceedings," in April 1861 he called forth "the militia of the several states of the Union, to the aggregate number of seventy-five thousand to . . . maintain the honor, integrity, and existence of our National Union."[29] The governors of the Northern states responded enthusiastically, assembling militias, or state armies, to march immediately to Washington, D.C. Within a month, well before Lincoln had decided on a military course, the governors of Northern states were shipping volunteers to Washington in numbers far exceeding the presidential request. By December 1861, over 640,000 men had volunteered for military duty in the North. There was only one problem: most of

them had not had a single day of military training.

Without these volunteers, the U.S. Army in 1861 numbered only sixteen thousand men, and only a handful of them, most of

Where Have All the Farmers Gone?

When President Lincoln made his first call for volunteers to the Union army in April 1861, a huge number of able-bodied men from farms and rural communities responded. Although farm women eventually took up the slack, many farms looked abandoned during that first summer of the war. The September 27, 1861, edition of the Bucyrus Journal *in Bucyrus, Ohio, reported that the shortage of farmers was also evident at the 1861 county fair. This excerpt is taken from George Winston Smith and Charles Judah's* Life in the North During the Civil War.

"The Fair last week was in one particular a success, and in another, a failure. Financially, it was a success, as the attendance was almost as large as usual, and the receipts sufficiently large to pay the current expenses—a result unlooked for this year. But the exhibition was a failure. A number of those who have heretofore taken an interest in the institution, were opposed to holding a Fair this season, and after it had been decided to hold it, instead of assisting to make it what it should be, threw cold water upon the enterprise, from as many pipes as they could control. The impression got abroad that it was doomed to be a failure, and of course it was. The exhibition of stock was very light, the mechanical department was almost nothing. Floral Hall was ditto, and the exhibition of Fruits and Vegetables very slim."

Northern men of all ages rushed to enlist in the U.S. Army, hoping to preserve the faltering Union.

whom were near retirement age, had any wartime experience. To make matters worse, many of the best officers, graduates of West Point, the U.S. Military Academy in New York State, were Southern men, bred and raised in a tradition that valued soldiering as the profession of a gentleman.

In cities and towns across the North, however, businessmen, lawyers, politicians, even clergymen, stepped forward to accept commissions as officers of the volunteer regiments. Formed as state militia units, the soldiers of these regiments proudly referred to themselves as the Sixty-ninth New York, the Fifty-third Illinois, the Sixth Kansas, and so forth. Governors assigned officer positions to friends, political supporters, and men to whom they owed political favors. Rarely was any consideration given to one's military experience or skills. These officers, in turn, recruited soldiers from their hometowns and communities.

What they lacked in military science and experience, the new recruits attempted to make up in enthusiasm. Raising an army became a community-wide affair. Recruit-

ment fairs and picnics were held on main streets in small towns throughout the country. Print shops made posters; brass bands blared patriotic marches; and local ladies baked pies. Young men came forward by the hundreds, moved by the excitement of the moment, or by the fear of being called cowards. Each regiment consisted of ten companies, and each company had at least a hundred men, often recruited from a single neighborhood or town. Most companies elected their officers by popular vote.

The spirit of recruiters and recruits alike reflected a naive sense of adventure, as if the destination were some great sporting contest. Most of these early recruits signed up for a three-month term, and they expected to be home long before the three months were up. Indeed, many of the early recruits feared that the war would be over before they had a chance to fight. One after another, volunteer regiments descended on their state capitals, where they awaited orders to be sent to Washington, D.C. Trainloads of raw recruits poured into the nation's capital, until the city was virtually taken over by

New recruits in Philadelphia board trains destined for Washington, D.C. Many volunteers viewed the war with a naive sense of adventure.

mobs of unruly, undisciplined men in variously colored uniforms.

Forming the Army of the Potomac

Thus the Army of the Potomac was a fighting machine of inauspicious origin. It was nearly two years before either the North or the South managed to put the majority of their soldiers into the standard blue and gray uniforms that we normally associate with the Civil War. At first, companies wore uniforms designed by their local sewing committees, and some of them were extremely colorful. In fact, historian Allen Guelzo has labeled this early Civil War period "the war of the thousand colored uniforms."[30] The Seventy-ninth New York Regiment arrived in Washington wearing Scottish-style kilts. The Third Maine wore gray uniforms, which, until they switched, made them indistinguishable from the Rebel army. And then there were the numerous regiments that imitated the extremely popular and dashing "Zouave" uniforms of the French Algerians. They sported baggy red trousers, a short cutaway jacket in brilliant blue, and a red fez or turban. Unfortunately, at the beginning of the war, several Confederate regiments also wore the same Zouave uniforms.

For the leaders of the Union army, training such diverse regiments proved nearly impossible, especially since most officers had no more experience than the enlisted men under them. Training was often delayed while the officers stopped to consult military handbooks. In many camps, special night schools were held for inexperienced officers to learn what they would be expected to teach the men the next day. Sometimes officers would sneak into the woods at night to practice shouting commands at the trees. The men of the Fifth Wisconsin watched in amazement one day as their colonel, leading his first regimental drill, lost his notes in the wind. Uncertain what else to do, he dismissed the troops. "It is a rather funny operation," observed one of his soldiers, "for one man to teach another what he don't know himself."[31] A Pennsylvania infantryman

Private Francis Brownell of the Eleventh New York Infantry poses for a photograph in "Zouave" attire. These dashing uniform styles were popular during the Civil War, with soldiers from both sides sporting the Zouave fashions.

Little Soldiers

The war kindled the imaginations of children, which in turn sparked the ingenuity of children's toy and clothes makers. A wide array of replicas, from uniforms to toy weapons, became extremely popular. The Zouave uniform with its bright blue waistcoat, red balloon knickers, and tassled fez cap was probably the most popular uniform replica, although the standard blue cavalry officer's uniform, the personal favorite of President Lincoln's eight-year-old son, Tad, was also in great demand. Toy marching drums were nearly as popular as toy guns and sabers. Even educational books, such as alphabet books, often adopted a patriotic, war-related theme.

described his colonel's military knowledge this way: "Colonel Roberts has showed himself to be ignorant of the most simple company movements. We can only be justly called a mob and not one fit to face the enemy."[32]

In charge of this "mob" of soldiers, President Lincoln placed General Winfield Scott, a hero of the Mexican War, which ended in 1848. The general had plenty of knowledge and war experience to share with his officers. Unfortunately, he was seldom available in the field. Scott had not had an active commission for over ten years, and during that time he had gained so much weight that he could not mount his horse without the help of two men.

Nevertheless, the people of Washington, D.C., welcomed the Union army enthusiastically. For one thing, the influx of young men, many of them away from home for the first time, did wonders for the local economy—especially in Washington's numerous taverns and brothels. The leaders of most volunteer regiments apparently kept poor track of their troops, for the local newspapers often reported with dismay soldiers sighted in uniform on the city streets at the same time that their regiments were supposed to be drilling.

Fortunately for the Union, the better-disciplined Confederate army did not choose to attack Washington, D.C., in the summer of 1861. The leaders of the Confederate army viewed their mission as defensive: to protect the homeland against an invasion by the North, not to attack or occupy foreign soil. Meanwhile, many Northerners urged President Lincoln to do just that: invade the South and occupy Virginia, especially after the Confederate army brought growing numbers of cannon and reinforcements to Manassas Junction, Virginia, only thirty miles southwest of Washington.

Finally, on July 21, 1861, a hot, muggy day in northern Virginia, thirty-five thousand soldiers of the Army of the Potomac, the largest American army that had ever been assembled, marched to Manassas and met the Confederate army along a small stream named Bull Run. Though it heavily outnumbered its enemy, the undisciplined and inexperienced Union army was soundly defeated at the Battle of Bull Run. The first major battle of the Civil War was a major disaster for the North.

When the battle ended, both sides withdrew in shock and horror at what had taken place. That night, there were bodies, some without limbs or heads, strewn across the battlefield. Scattered here and there among the dead, hundreds of seriously wounded Yankees and Confederates writhed in pain, called for help, or begged for water. The survivors on both sides, for the most part, were too appalled by the eerie sights and sounds of the night to go to the aid of their fallen comrades.

With the Battle of Bull Run, the Civil War had begun in earnest. There was no turning back now, though observers realized

General Winfield Scott (flanked by his officers) was given command of the U.S. Army. Despite Scott's war experience and tactical knowledge, he often left his officers to flounder for themselves in the field.

Union and Confederate forces face off at Bull Run during the first battle of the Civil War. The four-year-long war would prove to be the bloodiest in America's history, claiming the lives of over 620,000 Americans.

that the war was not going to be a brief adventure. Yankee soldiers who had expected to be welcomed home by Thanksgiving now faced the grim reality that they would be extremely lucky to be home alive for Christmas. Still, no one in the North believed that they would be at war nearly four years later, and no one would have guessed that before it was over, approximately half of all young men in the North between the ages of eighteen and thirty would see action, or that 620,000 Americans would die in battle, more than the combined deaths from all the other wars the United States has fought.

Life in a Union Army Camp

Between April 1861, when the Civil War began, and April 1865, when it finally ended, over one million Northern men served in the Union army. While the soldiers camped, marched, and fought, their parents, wives, girlfriends, brothers, sisters, and friends awaited their letters from the front. In the long intervals between letters, family members followed the events of the war obsessively. Maps were spread on parlor tables in most homes, with pins marking battle sites and ink lines tracing the movements of loved ones' regiments. The daily life of the soldier in a Union army camp was a matter of grave con-

cern, not only for the enlisted soldiers, but for the great majority of Northerners.

Camp Population Reflects Population of the Union

The typical Union camp housed men of all economic classes and nationalities. Nearly half the Yankee soldiers had been farmers. The remainder came from a wide variety of occupations, which lent a remarkable versatility to the average regiment. When a weapon or piece of equipment needed repair,

Union soldiers relax on the bluffs above their campsite in this photograph from May 1862.

Men from diverse backgrounds and occupations formed the core of the Union army. The majority of these soldiers were single white Protestants between the ages of eighteen and twenty-nine.

someone in camp knew how to fix it. Soldiers with experience in working on railroads and bridges were also easy to find, as were carpenters who could build winter huts for the officers.

Of course, the officers, who ate and slept in the dry, warm huts, tended to be from the upper and middle classes. The infantrymen, who shared blankets, slept in makeshift tents, and stretched their rations of jerky and dry biscuits until their stomachs groaned with hunger, tended to come from families of laborers and farmers, often immigrants. One out of four Union soldiers was a first-generation American.

To recognize the important contribution of the immigrants, and to encourage more of them to enlist, President Lincoln gave general's commissions to several well-known citizens of foreign birth. More than 200,000 Germans served in the Union army. New York, Ohio, and Wisconsin furnished several regiments that were almost totally German, and several regiments from other states had German majorities. The next largest immigrant contingent was Irish. More than a dozen regiments from New York City alone had Irish majorities. One regiment, the Fifteenth Wisconsin, was all Scandinavian. In its ranks were 128 men named Ole.

Still, the majority of Yankee soldiers were white, Protestant, and native-born. Most were young and unmarried. Four out of five were between the ages of eighteen and twenty-nine. And among those who did not fit in this age group were thousands who were younger than eighteen. Officially, eighteen was the minimum age for enlistment, but many boys lied about their age, and many recruiters ignored the age requirements. For musicians and drummers, there was no minimum age, and photos from Civil War camps show

Feeding an Army

In his book The Civil War: Tenting Tonight, The Soldier's Life, *James I. Robertson describes the typical diet of a Union soldier.*

"The official daily ration for one Union soldier was 20 ounces of salt beef or 12 ounces of salt pork; more than a pound of flour; and a vegetable, usually beans. Coffee, salt, vinegar, and sugar were also provided. Although this was plenty of food, it left much to be desired in taste and freshness. The meat was heavily salted in a pickling brine so that it could be preserved for two years at outdoor temperatures in all seasons. This 'salt horse,' as the men called it, was so salty that it had to be soaked in water to make it edible. The soaking process leached many of the nutrients out of the meat along with the salt.

When in the field, the men saw little beef and few vegetables. They survived on salt pork, dried beans, hardtack, and coffee. The pork and beans, and bread when available, was usually fried in gobs of grease, a practice that resulted in numerous digestive ailments. Hardtack was probably the single most despised article in the soldier's ration tin. Shaped like a cracker, three inches square and about half an inch thick, hardtack was a biscuit made of flour and water. It was so hard that it earned a number of nicknames, such as 'teeth-dullers,' and 'sheet-iron crackers.' Because they could hardly break off a piece of hardtack and chew it, the men often soaked the crackers in water and then fried the mess in grease, creating a dish they called 'hell-fired stew.'

Hardtack also had another nickname: 'worm castles.' For as hard as these biscuits were, they seldom arrived in camp without first being infested with maggots and weevils. As one Yankee soldier wrote in a letter to his family, 'All the fresh meat we had come in the hardtack, and I, preferring my game cooked, used to toast my biscuits.'"

numerous examples of nine- and ten-year-old drummers and buglers marching behind their companies. A surprising number of older men also signed up. The oldest on record was Curtis King, who enlisted in the Thirty-seventh Iowa Infantry at the age of eighty. King's regiment, which was known as the Graybeards, boasted 145 soldiers aged sixty or older.

Unsanitary Conditions

Early in the war, gung-ho volunteers of all ages came to the Yankee camps. But a typical Union army camp was enough to dampen the enthusiasm of even the most naive and idealistic recruits. Most often, several regiments camped together in enormous camps of more than five thousand soldiers. Huge tents, which held as many as twenty soldiers per tent, were arranged in long rows, like the streets of a city. In wet weather, the feet of marching soldiers, the hooves of horses and mules, and the wheels of cannon carts and supply wagons turned these streets to streams of soupy mud. In summer, the mud turned to dust. As one Connecticut infantryman noted, "One's mouth will be so full of dust that you do not want your teeth to touch one another."[33]

There was little sanitation in the camps. Long trenches were dug for latrines, and garbage was usually piled in large mounds. On hot, summer days, the putrid smell of waste and rotting garbage that attracted hordes of flies and mosquitoes made camp life miserable. The enlisted soldier could not escape the heat, the stench, or the annoying bugs. Inside the tents, the atmosphere was, if anything, worse than outside. While flying insects droned incessantly, ants crawled about the ground. On cold or rainy days, when the tent flaps had to be kept closed, the stagnant air inside the tents reminded the soldiers of their uncomfortably close quarters. John D. Billings, an artilleryman from Massachusetts, remembered the experience years later, but with little nostalgia:

> To encounter the night's accumulation of nauseating exhalations from the bodies of twelve men (differing widely in their habits of personal cleanliness) was an experience which no old soldier has ever been known to recall with great enthusiasm.[34]

The only time the soldiers welcomed the idea of sharing a tent with eleven or twelve other men was on a winter campaign, such as the one Union general Ambrose Burnside led against the Confederate army at Fredericksburg, Virginia, in December 1862. Each soldier had been issued only one extra blanket and a wool coat, scant protection indeed against the snowstorms that blew across northern Virginia. Most regiments erected their camps so as to use natural hillside terrain as a shield against the wind. The highest-ranking officers were provided with makeshift log cabins, and company sergeants and corporals often ordered their infantrymen to build dugout shelters in the hillside, but the soldiers' tents were still pitched on the cold, wet ground.

Winter campaigns were rare, however, as most generals used the winter months to train reinforcements and new recruits, and to

Despite snow and freezing temperatures, volunteers in the Army of the Potomac line up for training during their winter break.

replenish their supplies. On whatever land they occupied, the regiments built semipermanent winter camps—miniature cities of log huts. While the soldiers still slept on the cold ground, the drafty, dark, damp huts offered far more warmth and comfort than the standard army tent. One soldier described the spring, which brought orders to break camp and return to battle, as "the demon [motivating force] of all our ease and happiness."[35]

Daily Life in a Typical Union Company

A typical company comprised a captain, one first and one second lieutenant, a first sergeant and four lower sergeants, eight corporals, two musicians, a wagoner, and eighty-two privates. Beyond the officers and men of his own company, as a rule, a soldier would recognize by sight the commissioned officers of his regiment, which consisted of ten companies. These officers included a general or colonel, a lieutenant colonel, a major, an adjutant, a quartermaster, a physician (called a surgeon), an assistant surgeon, and one or two chaplains.

But it was the company's first sergeant who dominated a private's daily life. Every day, at 5:00 A.M. in the summer and 6:00 A.M. in the winter, the soldiers rose to the bugler's reveille and dragged themselves to roll call, lining up in front of a row of tents in the half-light of early dawn. Since inspections were not held at morning roll call, the soldiers slouched in meandering lines. Some wore boots, while others were barefoot. Some had put on their uniforms, while others wrapped themselves in bed sheets and linens.

After a breakfast of dry biscuits and coffee, the companies assembled for drills. As many as ten hours per day, the soldiers marched in formation, rehearsed commands, and reviewed what to do in specific battle situations. One private, Oliver Norton of the Eighty-third Pennsylvania, gave his impression of the routine: "The first thing in the morning is drill. Then drill, then drill again. Then drill, drill, a little more drill. Then drill, and lastly, drill."[36]

It took a lot of hard work to maintain an army in the field, so between drills, soldiers were kept busy building roads or laying pathways of pine logs, digging trenches for latrines, feeding and caring for the horses and mules, or chopping wood for cooking and heating. For some recruits, the hard labor came as quite a shock. Wrote sixteen-year-old Private Elbridge Copp of the Thirty-fourth New Hampshire:

> Men who at home were accustomed to nothing more strenuous than the handling of a yard stick and dry goods from over the counter, or light clerical work, lawyers, book keepers, school teachers, and among them were men of wealth, now find themselves as privates in the ranks subject to the orders of superior officers, doing the work of porters and laborers in all kinds of necessary drudgery.[37]

A dress parade and inspection for each regiment usually occurred after the last drills of the afternoon. These were followed by dinner, around 6:00 P.M., and afterward those who were not assigned to guard duty enjoyed a couple of hours of free time until lights-out at 9:00 P.M. Except when marching deep in Rebel territory, where the number of supply wagons had to be reduced, the soldiers had ample food, although its quality was very poor and there was little variety.

Commerce Between Yankees and Rebels

While the threat of starvation was rare for Union soldiers, it was an almost constant condition for many Confederate soldiers during the last two years of the war. In fact, on numerous occasions, Northern and Southern troops camped so close together that many Yankee soldiers supplemented their meager soldiers' pay by sneaking out of camp and selling some of their rations to Rebel soldiers. Such informal encounters with the enemy were one of the peculiarities of this war. Soldiers on both sides often had a great deal in

Reporting the War

Subscription magazines were a relatively new idea in the 1860s, and one of the most popular magazines among Northern troops was *Harper's Monthly*. When a soldier received a copy of *Harper's* in the mail from a family member, the publication usually circulated through the whole company,

even though it was at least a month old by the time it reached the right camp. *Harper's* was probably the first magazine to provide close-up coverage of a war. It sent reporters to stay in the Union camps and follow them as they marched to battle. It even commissioned a little-known photographer named Mathew Brady to capture scenes from the Battle of Antietam on film. Photography was still very new in the 1860s, and the first films required long exposures. Consequently, most of Brady's battle photographs were gruesome scenes after the battle had ended. Nevertheless, Brady's work set a standard for stark realism in war photography. Although his photographic accounts of the war were extremely popular at the time, Brady and his work were quickly forgotten after the war. He spent the last few years of his life as a lonely invalid in the ward of a Washington hospital reserved for the poor. Today, at least one of his photographs appears in nearly every book about the Civil War.

Mathew Brady (pictured) captured the hardships and misery of the Civil War in his popular photographs.

Rebel and Yankee pickets trade coffee and tobacco during a break in fighting. Although commerce between the North and the South was prohibited and carried a hefty punishment, pickets ignored the ban in favor of the handsome profits.

common. In fact, a Yankee farmhand from Ohio might have more to talk about with a Rebel farmer from Kentucky than with fellow soldiers from the streets of Cleveland or Cincinnati. Many soldiers had relatives and friends who fought for the other side. Between battles, Northern and Southern pickets, or scouts, often exchanged messages or inquiries for their comrades.

The more enterprising pickets carried on a rather brisk business. Since trade between South and North was officially suspended, the soldiers' black market could turn handsome profits. Rebel soldiers rarely had adequate food or clothing, but one commodity that the Rebels possessed in ample supply, and the Yankees coveted, was tobacco. A Yankee soldier could trade a raincoat or pair of boots for about ten pounds of tobacco. Then, he could sell the tobacco to his Northern comrades for as much as five dollars per pound. Meanwhile, his Rebel trading partner could easily fetch one hundred Confederate dollars for the Yankee raincoat or boots. Though a soldier caught consorting with the enemy in this way could be court-martialed

and severely punished, many officers ignored this commerce altogether while others overlooked the illegal aspects but demanded a share of the profits.

Leisure Activities

Except for the few hours between dinner and lights-out, the soldiers' only leisure time was on Sundays, when they were often given most of the day to read, write letters, and rest. The most popular reading material, of course, was letters from home. Mail was delivered to camp once or, on rare occasions, twice per week, and the letters were often two or three weeks old before they reached the right camp. Along with their letters, many wives, parents, or other relatives sent an occasional photograph and copies of magazines. Subscription magazines like *Harper's Monthly* were a relatively new but extremely popular invention in the Civil War era.

Music was also an important part of camp life. In addition to the drummers, buglists, and flutists who were enlisted as musicians, many soldiers played guitars, banjos, violins, harmonicas, and tambourines. Many a wooden washtub was temporarily transformed into a string bass or a bass drum.

Soldiers also used their free time for personal hygiene. A soldier could generally count on finding at least one barber among his company who had either been in the trade before the war or happened to be handy with a pair of scissors and found an opportunity to make a few extra dollars on the side. How often the soldier washed his clothing depended on how often his company camped near a river or stream. Since each soldier was issued only one official uniform, complete with trousers, blouse, jacket, and boots, his clothes took quite a beating. Most soldiers did their own laundry and patching. They carried sewing kits, which they dubbed "housewives," and took pride in their sewing skills. One soldier boasted of patching his trousers "as good as a heap of women would do."[38]

Of course, a handful of soldiers in every company—mostly officers—had the resources to pay a laundress to do these chores for them.

The women who earned their living by following the regiments and doing such chores often doubled as field nurses. As a group, they also acquired an unsavory reputation for making money through prostitution. With thousands of restless young men who faced the peril of death almost daily, there was little that could be done to curb the prostitution business. The same was true of the sale of whiskey. To anyone familiar with camp life, the heavy drinking was easy enough to understand, as one Connecticut officer explained in a letter home:

If you could look into our tents, you would not wonder that consolation is sought for in whiskey. The never-ceasing rain streams at will through numerous rents and holes in the moldy, rotten canvas. Nearly every night half the men are wet through while asleep unless they wake up, stack their clothing in the darkness, and sit on it with their rubber blankets over their heads, something not easy to do when they are so crowded that they can hardly move.[39]

Most soldiers did their own laundry while living in the army camps. Only a few wealthy soldiers could afford to pay the laundresses who traveled with the troops to do their wash instead.

Life in a Union Army Camp

Friendly Competition

Card games of all kinds, but especially poker, were extremely popular among soldiers. The men seemed to relish any form of competion, as evidenced by numerous accounts of elaborate winter snowball fights, sometimes pitting entire companies against each other. Soldiers even invented games to take advantage of common campsite pests. After scouring one another for ticks and lice, the men often used the specimens they found to stage tick and louse races.

Treating the Wounded

There were never enough surgeons, nurses, or medical supplies in the camps to handle all the wounded. Typically, one surgeon and two assistant surgeons served an entire company of one hundred soldiers. Surgery itself was still crude in the 1860s, and in many cases may not have been much help. There was no knowledge of antibiotics such as penicillin, so the most effective way to treat a badly wounded limb was to amputate it and apply a tourniquet to stop the bleeding. This usually stopped the spread of infection caused by the lead bullets and invading bacteria and parasites. The only anesthetic available was chloroform, which deadened the nerves slightly and made the patient drowsy.

Many soldiers shot in the stomach or chest died from these wounds because, of course, there was no way to amputate the injured part. The proportion of soldiers wounded in the Civil War who did not survive was very high: sixteen out of every hundred wounded soldiers died from their wounds, and nearly half of those who lived lost at least one limb. In recent wars, such as the Vietnam War, in contrast, only one out of every four hundred wounded soldiers died.

Loss of life was extremely high during the Civil War. Despite surgeons' efforts to mend the wounded, their crude techniques and lack of effective medicines made it nearly impossible to save most injured soldiers.

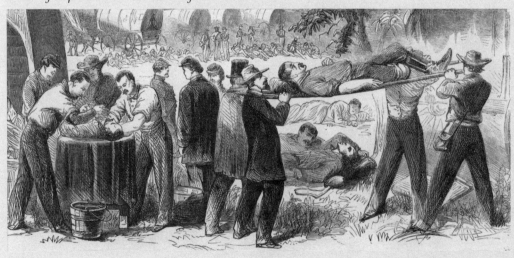

Soldiers gather around the camp sutler's tent, waiting to spend their earnings. The proprietors of these tents stocked everything from cakes and tobacco to blankets and boots.

Much of the enthusiasm for these games, of course, came from the gambling that accompanied them. On payday, immediately after receiving their pay, throngs of soldiers gathered for games of dice or poker. Jacob Hyneman, a soldier in the Union army who served under General Grant, wrote in his diary, "Only paid a week ago and have not a cent now, having bluffed away all that I did not send home. I don't think I will play poker any more."[40] Such sentiments were usually short-lived, however, as the heavy gambling continued seven days a week. A colonel with the Seventh Wisconsin noted with wry humor that the dice games invariably outdrew the chaplain's services: "I think this unfair, as the church runs only once a week but the game goes on daily."[41]

The gamblers who won did not have to go far to spend their money. As a forerunner to today's commissary, every regiment was accompanied by one government-approved vendor. In their tents, the vendors offered everything from cakes, pies, and tobacco to boots and blankets. Having no competition, they often sold goods at four or five times their actual value. Consequently, they acquired the name "sutlers," from a Dutch word meaning "to undertake low offices." A Northern newspaper correspondent wrote that sutlers were "a wretched class of swindlers and well deserved all their troubles."[42] Although sutlers often found themselves near, or even in, the battlefield, their greatest troubles came from disgruntled customers. Midnight raids on sutlers' tents were commonplace, and sympathetic officers often turned a blind eye to such activities.

Lincoln's Draft

In the last two years of the war, the character of the typical enlisted soldier changed. As the deaths, imprisonments, and casualties began to mount, the number of volunteers fell off sharply. In fact, it became necessary for President Lincoln to implement a draft. However, his Conscription Act, passed by Congress and signed into law in 1863, included a "buyout clause." Anyone whose name was drawn in the draft could pay three hundred dollars to the federal government to have a volunteer take his place. The government, in turn, offered a three-hundred-dollar bonus, or bounty, to anyone who volunteered to enlist. In addition, many cities, states, and private organizations offered their own bounties to volunteers. As a result, a volunteer could easily garner a thousand dollars by simply enlisting.

The practice of paying bounties drastically changed the complexion of the Union army. Men who were poor and unskilled seized this opportunity to get ahead. Meanwhile, many from wealthy backgrounds,

Volunteers swarm around a recruiting station that advertises a total bounty of $677 for new recruits. Wealthy Northerners who could pay $300 to the government were exempted from the draft. Their commutation fees were then given to poor recruits in the form of bounties.

especially those in manufacturing who were profiting greatly from the war, gladly paid their commutation fees and contributed bounties to the less fortunate fellows willing to take their place. One Northern veteran complained that the army had become a collection of "offscourings of northern slums . . . dregs of every nation . . . branded felons . . . thieves, burglars, and vagabonds."[43]

With these changes in recruitment, and with changing attitudes toward the war itself, Union army officers faced new problems. After their initial taste of battle, their first sight of bleeding, mutilated, dying comrades, thousands of would-be heroes fled their companies in terror. Desertion became so common—and so easy to get away with—that an entirely new type of Civil War soldier emerged: the bounty jumper. Bounty jumpers collected the valuable cash rewards for joining the army but had no intention of serving their full term. At the earliest opportunity, usually during the confusion of a battle, they slipped away unnoticed. Then, since no official identification document was required to enlist, many

bounty jumpers repeated the cycle over and over again, enlisting under another name, collecting another bounty, deserting, and reenlisting.

The Emancipation Proclamation: A Strategic Move to Weaken the South

After April 1862, when the first black soldiers were recruited, more than 130,000 black American men also fought for the Union. By 1862, President Lincoln had become convinced that defeating the Southern rebellion would require all-out war, in which the hostilities of the battlefield would be supplemented by a war aimed at the Southern economy and home front. Freeing the slaves and offering them safe harbor in the North would encourage Negroes to abandon the plantations, and it would leave slave owners without a workforce.

The effectiveness of this strategy became evident early in the war. Congress had already passed a law in May 1861 permitting

"A military hospital is no place for a lady." This was the opinion of most Americans at the start of the Civil War. From that perspective, even worse than work in a military hospital was being a field nurse. Traditionally, the women who volunteered their services to assist surgeons in the field were poor, uneducated, social outcasts. Some of them doubled as prostitutes.

The overwhelming need for medical aid in the Civil War began to change that situation. In the North, women like Clara Barton and Mary Ann Bickerdyke, fondly called Mother Bickerdyke, collected clothing, bandages, and medical supplies and brought them to the army camps. Bickerdyke, though she had no formal medical training, often comforted wounded soldiers in the field hospitals and even assisted in surgery. When one surgeon demanded to know by what authority she came to be in a field hospital, she replied, "I have received my authority from the Lord God Almighty. Have you any higher authority?"

The bravery of Clara Barton was legendary. In attending the wounded she ventured so close to the front lines that on one occasion, at Antietam, a stray bullet passed through her sleeve and killed the soldier she was caring for. After the war, Barton founded the American Red Cross Society.

Clara Barton's courage and compassion on the battlefield helped gain respect for female nurses and their profession.

the Union army to "confiscate all property, including slaves" that had been used in assisting the Confederate military. Word that the Union army took escaped slaves into its camps soon spread among slaves in the Southern states, and thousands made it to Union army camps, where they were declared free. In the summer of 1862, Lincoln decided to extend this declaration of freedom to all slaves in the Confederate states, believing that it would create havoc throughout the South and provide the Union with something it desperately needed: more soldiers.

When emancipation became official, in January 1863, Northerners were strongly

Recruiting Black Soldiers

Frederick Douglass, a former slave who escaped captivity and later bought his freedom, was one of America's most eloquent advocates of abolition and equal rights. He spoke so convincingly in favor of arming black soldiers and training them for combat that President Lincoln finally authorized the forming of several all-black regiments. Douglass and other leaders of the black community encouraged their fellow residents to enlist. In Philadelphia, an eight-foot-tall recruiting poster was addressed to the city's "Men of Color." As quoted here from J. Matthew Gallman's *The North Fights the Civil War*, the poster read:

> For generations we have suffered under the horrors of slavery, outrage, and wrong; our manhood has been denied, our citizenship blotted out, our souls seared and burned, our spirits cowed and crushed, and the hopes of the future of our race involved in doubt and darkness. But now our relations to the white race are changed. Now, therefore, is our most precious moment. Let us rush to arms!

Gallman also quotes from the diary of George W. Fahnestock, showing the less heroic, but typical, reason that most Northern whites supported the idea of blacks in combat:

> I only wish we had two hundred thousand blacks in our army to save the valuable lives of our white men.

Less educated whites voiced their support in crude verses, such as the following excerpt from a song that exhibits both its author's illiteracy and the bigotry of those who sang it. The song is quoted in Smith and Judah's *Life in the North During the Civil War:*

> Some tell us 'tis a burning shame
> To make the naggers fight,
> And that the thrade of being kilt
> Belongs but to the white;
> but as for me, upon my soul, So
>   liberal are we here,
> I'll let Sambo be murdered instead
>   of myself
> On every day in the year.

After fleeing the South, many young black men joined the Union army to help put an end to slavery.

At the beginning of the war, black soldiers served in separate, all-black companies in which they performed manual labor and demeaning chores.

divided over how to handle the great number of former slaves who began arriving in the North. One popular solution was to enlist as many young black men as possible in the army. Their treatment, however, reflected the inequality that was typical of Northern society. Black soldiers were assigned to separate, all-black companies, which were led by white officers. A few black soldiers did become officers, but they were seldom saluted or paid due respect by white enlisted men.

At first, black soldiers were not allowed to carry guns or enter combat. Many Union officers held racist notions that black soldiers lacked the discipline and courage to perform under fire. So blacks were put to work doing the most miserable and unrewarding jobs, such as digging trenches, building earthworks, and clearing battlefields of the dead and wounded.

Black Soldiers Prove Themselves in Battle

Sentiment gradually changed, however, especially as the war dragged on and casualties mounted. Frederick Douglass, born in slavery, later becoming perhaps the most eloquent spokesman for equal rights, argued endlessly for the use of black soldiers in combat. Douglass believed that this was an opportunity for blacks to prove to whites that they deserved not only freedom but the full rights of citizenship. "Once let the black man get upon his person the brass letters, U.S.; let him get an eagle on his button, and a musket on his shoulder and bullets in his pocket, and there is no power on earth which can deny that he has earned the right to citizenship,"[44] Douglass predicted.

By fighting in combat, Frederick Douglass believed blacks could earn both their freedom and U.S. citizenship.

The extraordinary Colonel Robert Gould Shaw was among the few Northerners who treated blacks with kindness and equality. Shaw was also the first commander to provide arms to his all-black regiment.

Most Northern whites who backed the push to arm black soldiers did not agree with Douglass that blacks deserved the right to vote or hold office. In fact, they just believed that more blacks, and fewer whites, should suffer the casualties of the war. President Lincoln himself used this argument: "Whatever Negroes can . . . do as soldiers, leaves just so much less for white soldiers to do, in saving the Union."[45]

Once black soldiers were allowed to fight, their performance quickly put to rest the racist misjudgments of their capabilities in combat. By the end of the war, 179,000 black men had served in 166 all-black regiments, and many of them performed heroically. Twenty-one black soldiers earned the Medal of Honor for valor above and beyond the call of duty.

Many Northerners were particularly interested in the exploits of the Fifty-fourth Massachusetts Regiment. This all-black regiment commanded by Colonel Robert Gould Shaw, son of a prominent white abolitionist from Boston, was the first to arm black soldiers. In July 1863, the Fifty-fourth was asked to lead an assault on Fort Wagner near Charleston Harbor, a particularly dangerous assignment. In the ensuing battle, nearly half the regiment was killed, including Colonel Shaw. As a way of disgracing the colonel, the Confederates buried him in a mass grave with his black troops. His family, however, replied that this was the most honorable resting place for an officer, with his men on the battlefield.

Though such a sense of equality was rare among Northerners, on the battlefield and in the trenches, the barriers between black and white, rich and poor, urban and rural, the divisions that lay at the heart of American life in the Civil War era, often disappeared in the desire to win a battle at all costs.

4

The War's Economic Impact

When the Civil War began, newspapers in the South were fond of reporting eyewitness accounts of economic disaster in the North. A reporter from the Richmond *Daily Examiner* who visited New York City described its "silent streets" and "deserted hotels." "The glory of the once-proud metropolis is gone," he wrote, "for the trade of the South will never return."[46] Many Northerners shared the view that the North depended so heavily on its trade with the South that when it stopped, the North's economy would crumble. Evidence from the early months of the war suggest that it almost did.

Financial Crisis Grips the North

The most serious problem was a shortage of cash and credit. Northern merchants had to write off over $300 million owed to them by Southern customers. Many Northern banks that had invested heavily in the cotton trade and made large loans to Southern cotton growers collapsed. The U.S. Treasury, saddled with the new debts of creating an army and financing a war, had lost the tax revenue of eleven former states.

The timing of the financial crisis could not have been worse for President Lincoln, who was just forming the first Republican administration in history. Business leaders who had been instrumental in electing Lincoln began to lose confidence in him. They

wondered seriously about the future of the nation itself. Could the government survive?

During these first few chaotic months, it looked as though the Union might lose the war by financial default. Lincoln had underestimated the strength and determination of the Confederate army. Along with his military and economic advisers, he initially expected the war to be over within six months. When that did not happen, the federal government found itself in an unprecedented situation: it

While President Lincoln was assembling the first ever Republican administration in the United States, his Union was facing financial ruin.

was $200 million in debt. As the new year, 1862, began, Salmon P. Chase, U.S. Treasury secretary, informed Congress that "the Treasury is nearly empty." At that time, the federal government did not print money as it does today; moreover, it was forbidden by law from making payments to debtors in paper bills. It could pay only "in specie," that is, gold and silver. Consequently, as the government tried to meet its payments to the businesses and banks that were its creditors, its supply of gold and silver coins dwindled rapidly.

Fearing that the federal government might default on its debts to institutions, many Northerners grew worried about the value of paper money, which was supposed to be backed by gold and silver reserves. At this time in American history, all paper bills, or banknotes, were printed by banks and other businesses, and, in some cases, by cities. By law, every enterprise that issued banknotes was required to honor the face value of its own notes, in specie, but it was not required to honor the full value of any other enterprise's banknotes. If, for example, you tried to exchange a five-dollar bill from the American Bank in Baltimore at another bank or at a business office, you might receive only two dollars and fifty cents in coins. Many Northerners panicked, rushing to banks to exchange their paper notes or withdraw their savings in gold and silver, which set in motion a vicious cycle. Many banks could not keep up with the demand and were forced to close. Many businesses raised their prices, fearing that they would not receive full value for the paper money used by their customers. In this uncertain climate, no one felt safe borrowing or investing money. "Never before perhaps in the history of this country," wrote the *New York Tribune*, "has such a feeling of uncertainty, of alternate hope and fear, prevailed in the business community."[47]

Consequently, the economy sputtered. Businesses not only demanded outrageous prices in devalued paper money but refused to hire new employees. Business was so bad that several large textile and shoe factories in New England closed down. In Michigan, iron production dropped 20 percent, putting many unskilled laborers out of work.

The economic calamity may have been felt most strongly in the Midwest, where farmers and merchants had dealt regularly with Southern buyers. The price of corn tumbled so low that some farmers burned their crops as fuel rather than sell it at a serious loss. Hog and beef prices fell to half their prewar levels. Citizens in midwestern states like Illinois, Indiana, Missouri, and Kansas spoke openly of following the example set by the Southern states, namely, of seceding.

During the Civil War, banknotes were backed by paper money rather than the usual gold and silver. This one-dollar note from Merchant's Bank in New York City was issued in 1862.

Yankee "Greenbacks" Spark the Economy

In February 1862, the Republican-controlled Congress reacted to the crisis by passing the Legal Tender Act. This act created, for the first time, a national currency, and it permanently altered the nation's monetary structure. It authorized the U.S. Treasury to print its own paper money, which was not backed by gold or silver, but was legal currency that could be exchanged with any other banknote at face value. Secretary Chase immediately put into circulation $450 million of these new "greenbacks."

As long as citizens could count on the federal government's staying in business, they could use paper money with confidence. Thus farmers began to borrow from banks to buy seed and fertilizer. Knowing that the government would need crops to feed the huge Union army, they borrowed and planted on a grand scale. There was only one problem: who would do the farming?

At some time during the war, one out of every three Northern farmers joined the Union army, and thousands of others left their farms to answer the demand for labor in the iron mills and mines. In fact, during the fall of 1861, in the first year of the war, many crops were not harvested and rotted in the fields. Then, many of the women whose husbands had become soldiers assumed the tasks of farm management. Mothers and older children took over the farmwork for their missing husbands and fathers. "Just take your gun and go," went a contemporary song, "for Ruth can drive the oxen, John, and I can use the hoe."[48] Tens of thousands of women did just that. An Iowa woman, writing to her husband on the war front, reported that "our hired man left to enlist just as corn planting commenced, so I shouldered my hoe and have worked out ever since. I guess my services are just as acceptable as his."[49]

A farmer rides atop his McCormick's mechanical reaper while harvesting his crop. McCormick's reaper and other modern farming equipment became popular during the Civil War because it saved farmers valuable labor.

New Technology to Meet Growing Demands

The growing number of women doing the plowing, planting, and harvesting may have contributed to advances in farming technology. Cyrus McCormick had revolutionized grain harvesting by inventing the mechanical reaper in 1831, and farm machinery had been improving for several years before the Civil War. Before the war, though, most farmers had been reluctant to invest in the modern equipment. They regarded the expensive new machinery as suitable for a wealthy farmer with lots of land, not for an average farmer with his sixty to a hundred acres. With the new conditions introduced by the war, however, more and more farmers took the risk of investing in labor-saving machinery. An 1862 article in the *Cincinnati Gazette* describes this change of attitude:

> A few years [ago], McCormick came to Cincinnati to manufacture his reapers. The idea then was, that they were suitable only for the large prairie wheatfields. It was the only agricultural machine we had, and it was met, as usual, by doubt and hesitation. . . . Since then we have

reapers, mowers, separators, sowers, drills &c., making a great aggregate of agricultural machinery, which does the work of more than three-fold the number of men, who (without machinery) would have been required to do it. Indeed, without this machinery, the wheat, oats, and hay of Ohio, in 1862, could not have been got in safely. Besides, this machinery, which was at first only intended for large farms, now operates on the smallest.[50]

In many cases, it was women, managing farms in their husbands' absence, who were the first to purchase and use the improved equipment. What they lacked in physical stature and strength, they made up for with new horse-drawn plows, mowers, and rakes. "The overall effect of mechanization," proclaimed the *Scientific American* in 1863, "was to make farming comparatively child's play to what it was 20 years ago."[51] In the same year, the *Merchants Magazine and Review* published this assessment of the new technology:

> At the present time so perfect is machinery that men seem to be of less necessity. Of all the labors of the field, mowing was

formerly deemed to be the most arduous, and the strongest men were required for it. We have seen, with the past few weeks, a stout matron whose sons are in the army, with her team cutting hay at seventy-five cents per acre, and she cut seven acres with ease in a day, riding leisurely upon her cutter. This circumstance is indicative of the great revolution which machinery is making in production.[52]

Making the work more manageable was probably not the biggest reason that farmers invested in the state-of-the-art machinery, however. The war had created a tremendous demand for their products, and the new technology dramatically improved their productivity. Farmers sought information about new fertilizers, select seeds, and other techniques to increase yields. Subscriptions to magazines such as the *Grange Review* and *American Agriculturist* doubled during the Civil War era. In April 1861, an article appeared in the *American Agriculturist* pleading with farmers to make every effort to increase production:

There is now every encouragement to cultivators, to increase the products of their fields to the last bushel, . . . whether those products be wheat, corn, barley, oats, beans, peas, potatoes, carrots, turnips, orchard fruits, or garden vegetables. . . . For the crops yet to be put in, a thorough preparation of the ground, a selection of good seed, with the application of the last shovelful of manure from the barnyard, poultry yard, etc., will all tell in cash next Autumn. . . .

Again, as we write, the sounds of martial music, and the gathering hosts of armed men that almost momentarily pass our window, betoken an impending war of no

small magnitude. . . . As one result, those who are not called from their homes to the service of their country will find more work upon their hands, which, with the increased demands upon their fields, will require greater skill and effort. . . .

The foreign demand will alone greatly stimulate the market for agricultural products, and enhance prices, thus affording means for liquidating debts incurred for land, and for implements, and other liabilities. . . . Let, then, every cultivator of the soil take hold with increased energy and confidence, and spare no effort of hands and brain to secure at least "one bushel more," either

A farmer and his son use traditional methods to plow their field. Farmers who remained on the home front found that their crops were in demand throughout the North.

Female factory workers fill cartridges at the Watertown Arsenal in Massachusetts. The Civil War was a boon for arms manufacturers who grew rich supplying the army with war matériel.

by tilling better than ever before, or by increasing the area under cultivation, or by both of these means.[53]

Most Northern farmers recognized the financial rewards of raising "at least one bushel more." As a result, farm production in the North rose during the last three years of the Civil War. In 1862, and again in 1863, the Union states alone grew more wheat than the entire country, including the South, had produced in the previous record year of 1859. In addition to feeding the Union's troops and the civilian population, Northern farms managed to double their exports to Europe.

Wartime Demands Fuel an Economic Boom

After the first year of the war, the economic calamity had been transformed into an economic miracle. Besides farmers, many other Northerners found new opportunities for making money. Aggressive investors took out loans to be able to exploit the tremendous demands for clothes, munitions, and food created by the Union army, the largest armed force the nation had ever assembled. Hundreds of textile, railroad, and steel milling plants were transformed into factories for manufacturing war materials—uniforms, boots, rifles, and artillery. They could barely keep up with the government's demands. By the fall of 1861, already twice as many men were in uniform as President Lincoln had anticipated. By the end of 1862, the economy of the North, fueled by wartime demands and plenty of government-secured paper money, began an unprecedented economic boom.

Arms manufacturers were only the most obvious to benefit from the war. Production of wagons, harness equipment, saddlery, and other materials for hauling and carting military gear skyrocketed. The army's constant demand for uniforms, boots, coats, and caps kept most textile factories filled. Even though the wages of the working class did not rise as quickly as prices, they did rise. With so many young men gone to war, any man, woman, or child who wanted to work could find a job. Irish, English, and German immigrants continued to flow into New York and Boston and, from there, spread to eastern cities and to the farms and mines of the western plains.

The Birth of the Oil Industry

Petroleum, or crude oil, was once so common beneath the land surface on this continent that it occasionally seeped up into caves and springs. A few reports that Native Americans had used it as a body ointment aside, it was considered a smelly, worthless substance. Until the 1850s, that is. Then several scientists discovered that oil, when applied between moving parts of a locomotive or other iron machine, helped lubricate the equipment, which then ran much more smoothly. It was found, as well, that oil could be burned as fuel in lamps. Suddenly, this seemingly useless substance became the most hotly marketed commodity in the world.

In the summer of 1859, an enterprising railroad conductor named Edwin Drake built the world's first oil derrick along Oil Creek, a small stream in northwestern Pennsylvania. After drilling down about seventy feet, he struck oil. Soon Drake was pumping, and selling, about twenty barrels of oil a day. When others heard of his success, they flocked to Oil Creek to try their luck. By 1861, there were seventy-four producing oil wells on Oil Creek.

The characters who quit their jobs and sank their life's savings into such speculation included one "Coal Oil Johnny," whose exploits became legendary. Coal Oil Johnny happened to inherit a farm that sat atop a large reservoir of oil. With an income of $2,000 a day from the drilling rights paid by oil companies, Johnny hired a minstrel troupe and private train. He amused himself by traveling around the country putting on minstrel shows wherever he felt like it. Eventually he spent his whole fortune, whereupon he took a job as a baggage agent with the railroad.

More lasting fortunes were of course made in the oil fields, including those of John David Rockefeller and Andrew Carnegie. Rockefeller built America's first oil refinery, which became the nucleus of Standard Oil Company. Carnegie made his fortune by investing in oil fields and in the railroads used to carry the oil from the fields to the refinery. To this day, Rockefeller Center and Carnegie Hall are two of New York City's best-known landmarks.

John D. Rockefeller, one of America's most successful entrepreneurs, gained fame and fortune in the oil industry.

"Yankee Ingenuity"

Wartime productivity reached all-time highs in practically every industry. Even the steady flow of immigrants was not enough to quench the need for labor. Some of this demand had to be met with old-fashioned "Yankee ingenuity," or invention. Among the most important industrial inventions of the Civil War era was the sewing machine. Isaac Singer produced the first Singer sewing machine in 1851, but it took the demand for instantly delivering hundreds of thousands of Union army uniforms to compel clothing manufacturers to buy the machines and install them in their factories. Between 1860 and 1865, the number of

The front page of the November 1, 1851, edition of Scientific American *shows diagrams of Isaac Singer's revolutionary sewing machine.*

sewing machines in use in this country doubled. Similarly, the need to supply thousands of troops with boots helped Lyman Blake's invention of a shoe-stitching machine gain acceptance. Blake's machine and the demands of war combined to transform the shoe-making craft from a single-family, handcraft operation into a mass production industry. Unfortunately for Blake, he was better at inventing than at asset management. He sold his patent for a few thousand dollars to an investor—who was collecting $750,000 a year in royalties before the war ended.

Several Northern industries profited by providing substitutes for products that had been abundant before the war but were no longer available. In the absence of Southern cotton, woolen mills enjoyed a boom. Cotton rag was also an important ingredient in the manufacture of paper, so manufacturers who found substitutes like straw, wood pulp, and cornhusks made tremendous profits. Most trade between America and the Far East had gone through Southern ports, so the supply of such staples as coffee and sugar was severely cut. As a result, Northerners began producing sweeteners made from maple syrup, and coffee manufacturers blended chicory seed with coffee beans.

Other profitable industries included those that produced lumber, alcoholic beverages, and farm machinery. One indication of the boom in manufacturing during the war was the increase in factories. In Philadelphia, a major manufacturing center, fifty-eight new plants arose in 1862 alone, fifty-seven more opened in 1863, and another sixty-three were built in 1864. Even the small city of New Haven, Connecticut, opened a half-dozen new factories in a single year.

Every railroad car and steamboat in the Northern states was packed with manufactured products, or the raw materials and sup-

Railroad cars at the massive Singer factory wait to transport newly manufactured sewing machines. The amount of freight hauled by railroad companies nearly doubled during the Civil War as Northern manufacturers increased their production.

plies needed to produce them. Shortages of labor and material kept the railroad companies from building as much new track or as many new cars as they did in the 1850s, but the number of passengers and the amount of freight nearly doubled, and the railroad companies' profits soared. In 1862 the stock of the sixteen largest railroads in the North was valued at $70 million. Two years later, the stock for the same sixteen railroads was worth $150 million. The *American Railroad Journal* called the year 1864 "the most prosperous ever known to American railways."[54]

"From Rags to Riches"

Despite all its horror and destruction, the Civil War proved to be an economic boon to millions of Northerners. One financier,

quoted in *Harper's Monthly*, said, "The battle of Bull Run makes the fortune of every man in Wall Street who is not a natural idiot." The same *Harper's* article described the activity on Wall Street in the two years since the U.S. Treasury's issuance of $450 million in greenbacks:

Paper money brought every one into Wall Street, and interested every family in the ups and downs of stocks. It circulated like fertilizing dew throughout the land, generating enterprise, facilitating industry, developing internal trade; the railways found their business increase beyond their most sanguine [optimistic] expectations; dividend-paying roads had extra profits to divide; embarrassed [penniless] enterprises cleared off their debts, and became lucrative [very profitable] to

Samuel Colt: The Man Who Armed the Union

In 1854, in Hartford, Connecticut, Samuel Colt built the world's largest and most modern gun factory. A huge steam power plant in the center of the factory drove its machinery. In the spring of 1861, soon after Abraham Lincoln had been elected president, Colt foresaw the threat of war—and the opportunity to capitalize on it. He wired his factory superintendent: "Run the armory night and day with double sets of hands. I had rather have an accumulation of our arms than to have money lying idle."

Colt did not need to worry about weapons piling up, unsold. Over the next four years, he sold nearly three hundred thousand rifles to the Union army, and his name became almost synonymous with the revolver and pistol that he patented.

An aerial view of Samuel Colt's expansive gun factory, which was considered the world's largest and most modern operation when it was built in 1854.

their owners; every body wanted to own railway property. . . .

It is keeping within bounds to say that $250 million was realized as profits by operators in stocks between 1862 and 1864. . . . The profit was divided among many thousands of people. In 1863, and in the first quarter of 1864, everybody seemed to be speculating in stocks. Nothing else was talked of at clubs, in the streets, at the theaters, in drawing-rooms. Ladies privately pledged their diamonds as margin with brokers, and astonished their husbands with the display of their gains. Clergymen staked their salary, and some of them realized in a few months more than they could have made by a lifetime of preaching. One man, who had nothing in the world but a horse, sent him to a broker's stable and persuaded the broker to buy him a hundred shares; he drew from the broker, a few months after, a balance of $300,000.[55]

There were many such "rags to riches" success stories. The Civil War era marked the rise of many of America's richest and most famous families, including the Carnegies, the Rockefellers, and the Morgans. The story of dry goods merchant Alexander T. Stewart is another case in point. Stewart was one of hundreds of enterprising immigrants who realized the American dream. Arriving in New York from Ireland in 1837, Stewart was penniless but determined and, more importantly, shrewd. Starting as a tailor and a street merchant, he began buying and hoarding raw cotton around 1860. By the time the war broke out and the cost of cotton went through the roof, Stewart was the most visible and effective cotton broker in the Union. In 1862, he opened the nation's first department store, and by 1864, he reported an annual income of $4 million.

Compared to most in the retail industry, Stewart was a generous employer. Most of his employees earned close to the national average annual income of $1,000. Other employers were not nearly so generous.

A Widening Gap Between the Capital and Working Classes

For the most part, the rapid transition of the Northern economy helped the entrepreneurs who owned or invested in business. Indeed, great communication and transportation monopolies were founded during the Civil War era. By 1866, for example, Western Union had bought or driven out of business every other company in the booming new telegraph industry. The trend toward monopolies could also be seen in the forming of large interstate railroad companies and banks. The handful of Americans who controlled these corporations acquired extraordinary economic and political power.

While the families of inventors, investors, and business owners enjoyed their prosperity, the gap between rich and poor widened during the Civil War. Among the lowest paid workers were seamstresses, who were paid by the piece. A New York seamstress earned four cents apiece for sewing undergarments. Even using a sewing machine, she could produce only about seven pairs a day, working fourteen hours. In a week, she earned less than two dollars. In 1863, women umbrella makers went on strike for a raise from six cents per umbrella to eight cents. In an average eighteen-hour day, a woman could make a dozen. Obviously, there was no such thing as a federal minimum wage law, and the working class had virtually no power. Labor

A. T. Stewart, who rose from penniless immigrant to wealthy merchant, symbolizes the American dream. In 1862, he opened the first department store in the United States.

Operators work around the clock at the Western Union telegraph company. This communication giant dominated the industry by 1866.

unions and the practice of collective bargaining were attacked as unpatriotic. Strikes were put down by federal troops. Workers' resentment mounted, but under the circumstances constructive protest was impossible.

New Capitalists Face Mounting Criticism

Along with resentment of the captains of the new economy came a lament for the passing of the old-fashioned craftsmen—the furniture makers and cabinetmakers, the tanners and leather workers, the shoemakers and tailors. Many Americans criticized the new manufactured goods as "shoddy." The new manufacturers, they claimed, had no pride in product quality. Their only interest was in making money and spending it conspicuously. An editorial in the *New York Herald* in 1864 captures the resentment of many Americans toward the new rich and their ostentatious lifestyle:

The individual who makes the most money—no matter how—and spends the most money—no matter for what—is considered the greatest man. To be extravagant is to be fashionable. . . .

The world has seen its iron age, its silver age, its golden age and its brazen age. This is the age of shoddy. The new brownstone palaces on Fifth Avenue, the new [carriages] at the Park, the new diamonds which dazzle unaccustomed eyes, the new silks and satins which rustle over loudly, as if to demand attention, the new people who live in the palaces and ride in the carriages and wear the diamonds and silks—all are shoddy. . . . They live in shoddy houses. They ride in shoddy carriages, drawn by shoddy horses, and driven by shoddy coachmen who wear shoddy liveries [uniforms]. . . . They wear shoddy clothes purchased from shoddy merchants, who have erected mammoth stores, which appear to be marble but are really shoddy. They . . . fondly imagine

The Excesses of the New Rich

In 1864, an article in Harper's Monthly *compared the expenditures of the "nouveau riches," or new rich, with the excesses of the mad Roman emperor Caligula. The article has been excerpted in George Winston Smith and Charles Judah's* Life in the North During the Civil War.

"The suddenly enriched contractors, speculators, and stock-jobbers [speculators who specialized in stocks] . . . are spending money with a profusion never before witnessed in our country, at no time remarkable for its frugality. Our great houses are not big enough for them; they pull them down and build greater. They, like the proud and wanton [irresponsibly extravagant] Caligula, construct stables of marble at a fabulous cost, in which their horses are stabled (some, doubtless, to be fed on gilded oats), with a luxury never hitherto indulged in by the most opulent of our fellow citizens. . . .

It is not surprising to find the boundless extravagance of the times assuming forms at variance with propriety and taste. Parties, provoked to excessive folly and wild extravagance . . . have . . . invented a grotesque kind of fancy ball. In this the guests represent things instead of persons. . . . Last winter, during which high carnival was held by our *nouveau riches*, a dame got up one of these grotesque fancy balls. She herself appeared on the occasion as music, and bore upon her head an illuminated lyre [stringed instrument] supplied with genuine gas, from a reservoir and fixtures concealed somewhere under her clothes. 'We don't feel this war,' they say."

During the Civil War, the newly rich in the North continued to lead extravagant lifestyles.

themselves *à la mode de* Paris, when they are really *à la mode de* shoddy. . . . They are shoddy brokers in Wall Street, or shoddy manufacturers of shoddy goods, or shoddy contractors for shoddy articles for a shoddy government. Six days in a week they are shoddy businessmen. On the seventh day they are shoddy Christians.[56]

The *Herald* may have exaggerated, but often the "shoddy" charge was justified. Many Northern entrepreneurs made their fortunes by overcharging the government for arms or supplies. Union army uniforms were notoriously poor in quality. Investigating charges that local merchants were selling the government shoddy goods, the New York Chamber

Northern manufacturers of Union army uniforms overcharged the government for their poor quality goods. Many boots and uniforms fell apart long before the war ended.

of Commerce found that some merchants had supplied the army with boots whose soles were made with pasteboard and wooden shingles. One manufacturer was blamed for delivering a shipment of boots whose soles fell off after a half-hour's march. The manufacturer responded by claiming that those boots had not been intended to be marching boots. They were meant to be used by cavalry troops mounted on horses, not by infantry! An agent of the Union navy was caught in a scheme to bilk the government out of millions of dollars. The agent would purchase vessels that he knew were unseaworthy and sell them to the navy for twice what he had paid.

Perhaps the most amazing story, though, was the deal in which a speculator named Arthur Eastman bought a large quantity of old but still serviceable rifles from the War Department for $3.50 apiece. Eastman then sold the rifles to another speculator, Simon Stevens, for $12.50 apiece, and Stevens turned around and sold the whole lot back to the army for $22 a rifle!

The railroad industry also had its share of corruption and shoddy deals. Many railroad companies were accused of knowingly risking lives and property by using old, worn-out track, sagging bridges, and unsafe cars and engines. An 1865 editorial in the *New York Daily Sun* claimed that railroad accidents had become so common that its printers kept the headline "Awful Railroad Disaster!" ready for immediate use. The article went on to list a series of accidents over a two-month period in which four hundred passengers had been killed or injured. Then the author of the editorial offered his explanation for so many accidents:

We could name half a dozen railroads upon which a man has less chance for life and limb in a fifty-mile trip than our soldiers had in the battles of the Wilderness. The prevalence of old engines and rickety cars are clear evidence that the railroad companies have been in too great a hurry to grow rich.[57]

The "New Rich" Flaunt Their Wealth

The class of "new rich" that emerged in Northern cities was criticized for its tasteless expenditures, its costly entertainments, and its callous attitudes toward the rest of the community. Understandably, the labor class, at whose expense many fortunes were indeed made, questioned the humanity of an economy that permitted such disparity between owner and worker. However, criticism of the "new rich" also came from old New England families who could trace their ancestry back to the original colonists. There was a general though unconfirmed impression that members of the old, established families used their wealth with greater restraint and social responsibility. Many of the men from these families, who took military assignments as regimental commanders and also contributed a good deal of their own money in support of the war effort, severely chastised the wealthy financiers among them who paid $300 to avoid military service. Along with wealth, the old families claimed, comes social responsibility. To have fun and flaunt one's money while the nation was at war seemed immoral.

Undoubtedly, many of the new rich were just as committed to the war effort as any of the old families. And it is equally likely that some of the young men from proud Puritan stock found ways to skirt their military duties, too. Yet the perception and attitude persisted that the new industrial, urban economy was eroding the values traditionally found in rural communities across the North.

Life in the Rural North

In 1860, approximately half the entire Northern population lived on farms. Although this percentage had dropped with the influence of industrialization and urbanization, agriculture was still, by far, the North's biggest employer. Including the transportation and sale of food, plus the production and marketing of farm equipment and supplies, easily three out of every four Americans earned their living from agriculture.

A "Typical" Rural Community

Approximately half the families that lived on farms owned the land they worked. The other half rented the land and paid their rent as a share of all that they produced—usually one-third. Often the most prosperous farming families had inherited their land, so they had no mortgage obligations. Many who had mortgage payments to make were forced to supplement their income by working part-time as farmhands for others. Farm women often took in sewing, in addition to their daily chores.

The size of the average farm in 1860 was 150 acres, but that does not adequately reflect the great variety of Northern farms, from the average 25-acre vegetable farms of New England to the 300-acre dairy farms of Ohio, the vineyards of California, the wheat farms of North Dakota, and the cattle ranches of Wyoming. Farms differed in crops and products, in climate and soil conditions, and in methods of management. Nevertheless, one can draw some insightful generalizations about the "typical" farm community of the 1860s and the family farms that surrounded it.

Nearly half of all Northerners lived on rural farms during the antebellum years.

Regardless of the nature of its main crop, the typical farm family also grew most of its own food. From the garden and orchard near the house, the family could harvest enough potatoes and apples for home use and usually extra to sell to passersby. The family usually kept four or five cows, a horse or two, a few pigs, some chickens, and occasionally a small flock of sheep. They produced their own milk, butter, and cream; butchered beef, pork, and mutton; and tanned leather and spun wool.

The Hired Help

The more prosperous farming families were clearly distinguished by the addition of a hired man and a hired girl. The hired girl, quite often the daughter of a neighbor, earned, on average, $1.25 per day, plus room and board. She worked year-round, mostly indoors helping the farmer's wife. If asked to do extra work outdoors, such as milking or pitching in with the harvest, she often received additional pay. In addition to five or six major holidays, the hired girl took most Saturday afternoons off and all day Sunday, which she usually spent visiting her family.

There was more than enough work indoors for both the mother and the hired girl. After breakfast, they cleaned the kitchen, made beds, emptied chamber pots (for they did not have the comfort of indoor plumbing), washed, ironed, and mended clothes, baked bread and other pastries, and prepared meals, all without benefit of electricity or running water. Cooking and heating the house required loading potbellied stoves with wood and keeping the fires in them lit.

Unlike the hired girl, the hired man was not employed on the farm year-round. He usually stayed with the farmer's family from

A young girl helps her mother with the domestic chores by peeling newly harvested apples. Most rural families were self-sufficient, growing enough crops to provide for their families and selling the remainder.

April until November, the principal working months on the farm. During the eight-month work season, the farmer and his hand rose at about 4 A.M. and worked fourteen or fifteen hours a day. For $75 per month, plus board, the hired hand helped the farmer with plowing, seeding, splitting wood, hauling manure, building fences, repairing or constructing stables, and harvesting.

Caring for the livestock—feeding the animals, cleaning stables, milking cows, turning cattle out to pasture and bringing them back—occupied much of the hired man's time. In the summer, swarms of flies in narrow, ill-smelling stalls made milking the cows and other barnyard chores unpleasant. Rain sometimes brought a welcome day off for the hired hand, but more often the farmer recalled a porch rail that needed mending, a

A New England farmer and his farmhands gather pumpkins. During the harvest season, farmers often hired men to help with the chores and exchanged labor with their neighbors.

gate that had to be built, muck that was to be mixed with manure, grain to be threshed or cleaned, or apples to be ground into cider. Generally there was work for rainy days.

The hardest work, though, came at the beginning and the end of the work season with planting and harvesting. Planting began in April, in most Northern states, with plowing, rolling, pulling up stumps, burning refuse, and generally preparing the fields. In June, the farmer and his hired hand hauled great wagon loads of manure and spread it on all the fields for fertilizer. In July the harvest began in the hay and wheat fields. Even well-to-do farmers who owned a mower and a reaper had some fields or parts of fields that lay on steep hillsides, where the mowers and reapers could not go. These fields the farmer and his hired hand had to cut with a scythe, gathering the crop by hand. During harvest season, the farmer and his neighbors often "exchanged" labor, which allowed them to systematically clear the fields of every farm in the community.

Family Chores

Even during the "slack" winter months, there were plenty of chores to keep farm families busy. Fortunately for most families that could not afford a hired hand, the chores could be divided among several brothers and sisters. Everyone rose before dawn. While the older sons chopped wood and the younger ones cleaned the barn, their father spread clean straw on the barn floor and fed the milk cow and the plow horse. Meanwhile the daughters gathered eggs from the chicken coop, and the mother prepared a big breakfast. Steak, eggs, and apple pie constituted a typical breakfast, which the family sat down to eat at about 6 A.M., after the morning chores were finished. Following breakfast, the children bundled up and set out on the walk to their one-room country school, often a few miles from home.

The farming family had to work extremely hard, but if they had more good years than bad, without devastating droughts or hailstorms, free from grain-destroying weevils—and their crops brought good prices—they made a good income, which allowed them to live comfortably, but not extravagantly. They knew that for every year the crops were good, they could expect a bad year down the road. So they had to manage their money wisely and save enough to see them through the inevitable bad years—and to pay their debts, like the $20 monthly mortgage on their house.

A Spacious, Comfortable House

The moderately successful family farmer in the 1860s could afford to build a large, relatively comfortable house. Numerous advertisements in *American Agriculture* and other magazines told of lumberyards that would deliver the plans and all the lumber, joints,

and nails for $750. The new trend toward "balloon-frame" or "Chicago-style" construction had made spacious, two-story homes affordable for many middle-class families. Most farmers, with the help of neighbors who came to help on Saturday and Sunday afternoons, used such plans to build their own houses. Consequently, two-story farmhouses that were almost identical in everything but color and a few cosmetic touches dotted the rural landscape from Maine to Minnesota.

In almost every one of these homes, the showpiece was the front parlor. By the 1860s, wallpaper, inexpensive factory-made replicas of expensive handcrafted furniture, and other household goods were available. Middle-class families, eager to demonstrate their good taste to all visitors, decorated their front parlors to imitate those of millionaires. They could even purchase inexpensive prints of painted landscapes or portraits and hang them in wooden frames painted gold. By far the most popular of these prints, or lithographs, were created and sold by Nathaniel Currier and James M. Ives. Currier and Ives prints are still popular today, especially on greeting cards.

The lives of Northern farmers were consumed by work, and all members of the family were expected to perform certain chores. Even during the cold winter months, the farmers' sons were given tasks such as collecting and chopping firewood.

The typical parlor was perhaps only a third the size of the parlor in a mansion. But that rarely kept middle-class owners from trying to pack nearly as much furniture into them. As one interior decorating authority advised, "Providing there is space to move about, without knocking over the furniture, there can hardly be too much in the room."[58] A sofa, an overstuffed chair, and one or more small cushioned chairs provided sitting space. A marble-topped table generally occupied the center of the parlor and displayed an ornate family Bible or other valuable heirloom. A wooden bookcase and small desk usually stood along the wall. The wooden furniture was often elaborately carved with scrolls, claws, and brackets. Modest relief designs embellished the plaster ceiling. Carpets with diamond or square patterns covered the hardwood floors. Families that could afford a piano or organ usually placed it in the parlor.

Everywhere in the parlor one encountered pillows, doilies, knickknacks, family photographs, large and ornately framed mirrors, and, as space permitted, more knickknacks. The front parlor was often decorated and furnished to give the appearance of wealth, even at the expense of leaving the back rooms crudely furnished with homemade furniture. A contributor to *Harper's Bazaar*, a popular women's magazine, made this observation: "Was there ever an American woman who, furnishing a house, did not first lay aside the money for the parlor? A parlor must be, even if after it there comes the deluge [the great flood, prophesied in the Book of Revelations in the New Testament]."[59]

The second, or "back," parlor was typically more relaxed and informal than the front parlor. Here people felt comfortable removing their shoes, playing a game of checkers, singing songs, or taking a nap. Comfortable rocking chairs, chaises longues (reclining chairs), and overstuffed chairs filled this room. Cabinets held magazines, newspapers, children's games, sewing materials, and Father's pipes. A large oval table,

This prosperous New York farm boasts a large two-story home, typical of Civil War–era farmhouses.

New Farm Machinery

Many farmers and farmhands left their farms to join the Union army. To make up for the labor shortage and to meet the growing demand for food, Union farmers purchased the latest inventions in farm machinery, such as horse-drawn mowers and rakes. These machines had been invented in the 1850s, but it took wartime necessity to persuade most farmers to give up their traditional tools and methods. Also, because of the high prices farmers received for their products during the Civil War they could afford to lay out large sums for the new equipment.

The principle behind most of the new machinery was horsepower, literally. The plow, mower, or rake was mounted to a carriage and its rotating parts were connected to one of the carriage wheels by gear wheels. As the horse pulled, the carriage wheels turned, which caused the plow, mower, or rake to rotate. Often the machinery was first bought to help women and children work the fields in the absence of the men, but when the men returned, they often discovered that their wives and children had made their farms more efficient and productive than ever.

where family members could read, write, or play games, as well as eat meals, occupied the center of the room. Here the family took most of its meals and spent most of its leisure hours.

Beyond the back parlor stood the kitchen, with a back door that led to a rear, closed-in porch, where family members and hired hands could remove dirty denim overalls and boots. The kitchen itself was rather small, since it served as a place to prepare meals—not to eat them. It did not even contain a table, just a black cast-iron range along one wall that was flanked by countertops and cupboards. Open shelves filled with cooking utensils, spices, and canned goods lined two of the walls. The most modern style of iron range featured a large oven with wood-burning chambers on either side. When in use, the entire range was too hot to be touched without leather gloves or other protection. It not only baked, boiled, and roasted food, it was also one of the principal sources of heat for the ground floor. A large kettle or two of hot water for cooking or washing almost always sat on the stove top.

The second floor was divided into at least four bedrooms, two on either side of the hall. The two front bedrooms nearest the stairway were the largest, one of them being the master bedroom and the other usually housing a hired girl. The house was typically positioned so that the windows in the large bedrooms caught most of the morning sun, and dressing tables and mirrors were placed to take advantage of the morning light. Since the house contained no closets or private bathrooms, the large bedrooms were extremely useful. The furnishings in the master bedroom included a large wooden wardrobe, a chest of drawers, a washstand, and a small potbellied stove. This room served not only as a room for sleeping, but also as a room for dressing, sitting, and tending to personal hygiene. As in the kitchen, a kettle of water usually sat on the stove top, ready to be warmed for washing.

Sprucing Up for the Weekly Trip to Town

Without running water, personal hygiene usually entailed washing with a cloth dipped in warm water. Homemade bars of soap, made

An American Institution: The Saturday Night Dance

Every farming community knew how to prepare a barn or meeting hall for a Saturday night fling. This excerpt from Daniel E. Sutherland's The Expansion of Everyday Life, 1860–1876, *vividly re-creates an American institution.*

"They did not require large—or even proficient—bands. A lone fiddler would do just fine. 'It was a joy to watch him start the set,' recalled a Midwesterner of his county's star fiddler and caller. With a fiddle under his chin he took his seat in a big chair on the kitchen table in order to command the floor. One mighty stomp of his boot on the table top, a slicing sweep of his bow across the taut strings, and a command of 'Honors tew your partners—right and left Four!' and the dance began. . . . Revelers sang along to tunes like 'Miller Boy' and 'Skip to Ma Lou.' . . .

Even the lack of music seldom dampened spirits. 'The violin [fiddle] was taboo,' recalled one man of rural parties in his part of Indiana, 'but we sang songs and danced to them and hugged the girls until they would often grunt as we swung them clean off the floor or ground, in the barn or house on the green.' Among the favorite country dance songs, with or without fiddles, were 'Turkey in the Straw,' 'Irish Washerwoman,' 'Old Dan Tucker,' 'Billy Boy,' and 'Buffalo Gals.'"

from lye, probably generously scented with perfume, were the standard cleaning agent.

Saturdays were special days for the farm family. After morning chores were done, each family member bathed and dressed for "going into town." Except for special occasions and holidays, Saturday was usually the only day of the week on which the typical farm family bathed—and it really was a family affair. First a steel tub was hauled into the middle of the kitchen; then enough water to partially fill the tub was drawn from the outdoor pump and heated. One at a time, the family members would then soak in the tub, each person adding a little bit of fresh, warm water to the water already in the tub.

Once bathed, it was time to dress for going to town. For men and boys this was a relatively quick task. The most typical outfit included brown denim pants (the Levi Strauss Company began producing brown denims in the 1850s but did not introduce blue jeans until after the Civil War), a cotton or denim shirt in the spring and summer (wool in the fall and winter), a leather or wool vest, western-style boots, and a felt or straw hat. The only difference between this and the clothes worn all week was that the Saturday clothes were freshly laundered.

For the female members of the family, the grooming process consumed a bit more time. Long hair was in fashion, so the ladies had to first style their hair. The most common mode was to sweep the hair back into a cascade, which was secured with a bow or ribbon. Many women enhanced the thickness and length of their "fall" with a hairpiece, usually made from horsehair. They also experimented with various ointments and potions that promised to keep the skin smooth and youthful. A mixture of benzoin, honey, and alcohol, called "virgin's milk" was one favorite solution that was supposed to eliminate wrinkles and cleanse greasy skin. Finally, they sprayed or applied generous portions of perfume from head to toe.

Women and girls wore dresses almost exclusively, whether they were cleaning house, putting up vegetables, or going to town. With the exception of two or three fashionable crinoline-skirted dresses that were saved for Sundays, farm women's dresses were simple calico or gingham, worn long—usually to the ankles. Whether in public or just outdoors, women seldom were seen without a hat.

The General Store: The Heart of the Farming Community

For most rural families, the trip to town was an all-day, all-family affair. It was the one opportunity each week—in some cases only once every two weeks—to buy supplies for the family and for the farm. If the farmer had a broken wagon wheel or a plow to be repaired, he would drop the item at the local blacksmith's shop. Next, he might head for the tack and feed shop to buy oats for the horses. In the late winter or early spring, he would also buy seed to plant his crops. Before making these stops, however, he would probably take the rest of the family to the general store, and, after conducting his errands, that is where he would go to meet them.

The general store occupied a prominent, central location on Main Street. In fair weather, its broad, wooden porch held wooden rocking chairs and benches, which were usually filled by townsfolk who came to hear (or spread) the latest gossip. Like most buildings on Main Street, the general store was a simple, square-shaped, one- or two-story building, sometimes brick and sometimes wood frame. It usually had a large false front above the first floor, which protruded over the front porch and prominently bore the name of the establishment—typically nothing more elaborate than "General Store."

In inclement weather, people would gather inside the general store, usually on wooden stools or benches set around the potbellied stove. The store was typically cluttered and

Both employees and customers of this crowded general store take a break from their activities to pose for a photograph. Townsfolk from near and far gathered at the general store to purchase supplies and catch up on the latest town news.

crowded, somewhat like the typical family parlor. Lining the two side walls were shelf after shelf of tobacco jars, kitchenwares, crockery, bolts of cloth, bottles of whiskey, and sacks of flour, as well as canned goods, laundry soaps, medicines, clothing, school supplies, and any other daily needs of the rural family. Beneath some shelves were rows of drawers, in which one could find small items, like needles and thread, nuts, bolts, screws, and nails, stockings, suspenders, and fishhooks. In the center of the store, and running nearly its full length, were two long counters, on which the storekeeper displayed jewelry, ribbons, buttons, pipes, hair tonics, talcum powder, perfume, and other items. One of the counters usually held jars filled with assorted candies, cheeses, crackers, sausage, and other snacks for the hungry customer. Most grocery items, like rice, sugar, vinegar, crackers, lard, and salt, were stacked in barrels along the back wall. Overhead, harnesses, baskets, hats, and buckets dangled from the rafters. Other items such as wagon wheels, rope, farm tools, brooms, and mops were piled on the floor wherever there was room.

Besides offering the widest possible selection of groceries, clothing, and hardware, the general store usually served as the post office, the meeting place for local organizations, and the place where villagers gathered to hear the news. To sort out fact from fiction, people usually consulted the owner of the general store, who was among the town's most prominent citizens. If anything newsworthy was happening in the area, the storekeeper was the first to hear about it.

Community Spirit: A Nation of Joiners

Perhaps because their neighbors often lived more than a mile away, typical rural Northerners seemed to appreciate the opportunities they had to get together. Church groups and community activities enjoyed enormous popularity. Practically every middle-class adult male belonged to at least one fraternal or civic organization. Freemasons, Knights of Columbus, the Order of Odd Fellows, and a wide assortment of lodges—Elks, Moose,

The general store offered a wide variety of products, ranging from tobacco jars and bolts of cloth to harnesses and wagon wheels.

The Patrons of Husbandry, or the Grange as it was commonly called, was the largest farming organization in the nation. Men, women, and teenagers attended the Grange meetings and social functions.

Templars, and so on—fostered a wide assortment of elaborate rituals, handshakes, passwords, regalia, and hierarchies that gave members a sense of belonging. Most of these organizations had a strong civic spirit, too, as people took pride in building their cities and towns.

The single largest association of farmers in the nation was the "Grange," the common name for the Patrons of Husbandry. Nearly one million men, women, and teenagers belonged to the Grange. Some of them were poor "dirt farmers," while others were prosperous "gentleman farmers." The Grange distributed several regular publications with information about the latest trends and machinery. It offered loans and financial advice to farmers, and it endorsed the political candidates considered to be most sympathetic to farmers. But the Grange was especially popular because of its social activities.

In addition to regular monthly meetings, which usually took the form of berry-picking parties, barbecues, and picnics, most local granges organized three or four special social occasions each year. In the fall, after the harvest was in, the Grange celebrated Harvest Day with a weekend of dancing, singing, eating, and occasional prayers of thanksgiving. In the spring, Children's Day recognized the contributions of children to rural life, often by holding stock shows where children could show and sell their prize animals. Finally, no Grange social calendar would have been complete without an Independence Day parade and picnic.

As one might expect, the Fourth of July was the most exuberantly celebrated holiday in the North during the Civil War era. Nearly every town big enough to have a Main Street had a parade on the Fourth. Storefronts and houses alike were decorated with red, white, and blue bunting and national flags. This event was usually followed by a picnic, at which families gathered to eat fried chicken, potato salad, and watermelon. After hours of listening to patriotic and sentimental speeches by local politicians, the citizenry was ready for a smorgasbord of sporting activities: races, croquet, swimming, horseshoes, and baseball.

Pioneers Settle "the West"

While life on the farms and in the small towns of the rural North shaped the values of most Americans in the 1860s, the pioneer spirit also remained extremely strong. To many Americans, "the West" represented not only a

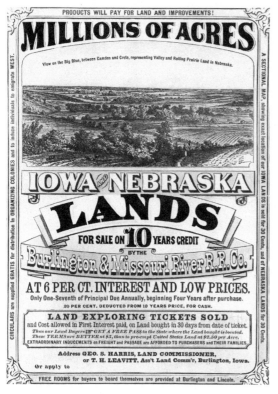

Circulars like this one, which advertises the sale of "millions of acres" in Iowa and Nebraska, were distributed across the country to entice people to migrate west.

geographic place but the idea of a vast, boundless frontier. Horace Greeley's famous admonition, "Go West, young man," was a kind of statement of faith—faith in the American work ethic and the seemingly unlimited potential for success. Indeed, most Americans in the 1860s referred to the midwestern states of Iowa, Nebraska, Wisconsin, Minnesota, and the Dakotas as "the West," so the territories to the west of these states must have seemed like an endless frontier.

Though it demanded great faith—some would say great naiveté—to pack up all one's belongings, load them into a covered wagon, and head for a destination one had never seen, the very fact that such an undertaking

was possible brought hope to many. The Civil War contributed to the westward expansion in several ways. Young men from eastern cities who had never left home before they joined the Union army returned from the war with a curiosity and a desire to explore that had been whetted by their travels. If they came from working-class families, they were not always content to resume employment at the factories or mines they had left behind. They had greater ambitions and, in many cases, they had greater savings. For about $750, one could buy a hundred-acre parcel of land in Minnesota, Wisconsin, or the Dakotas, along with all the tools and equipment to farm it. Many veterans returned from duty with that much and more saved up.

The war also contributed to a political climate that encouraged westward expansion. The North in general, and the Republican Party in particular, had long favored the idea of homesteading, or offering free, small parcels of western land to create opportunities for poor and middle-class Americans willing to work hard and support themselves. This initiative, of course, would undermine the opportunities of the wealthy landowners who wanted to buy up large tracts of western land. In fact, the greatest resistance to homesteading came from plantation owners in the South, who viewed the proposed arrangement, correctly, as a threat to the expansion of slavery. When the South seceded and left Congress in the control of Republicans, it opened the way to a National Homestead Act, which President Lincoln signed into law in 1862. The Homestead Act offered 160 acres of farmland to any American citizen willing to build a house on the land and farm it for at least five years.

The lure of free land drew hundreds of thousands of pioneers westward, but dreams of instant prosperity eluded most of them.

The Homestead Act

"Go West, young man!" Horace Greeley advised young Americans wanting to seek their fortune. In the Midwest and the West, the United States owned a fortune in land. Since its origin in 1856, the Republican Party had supported the homestead idea, granting this publicly owned land to American citizens willing to live on it and make it productive. In 1862 the Republican-controlled Congress passed the Homestead Act. According to the *Congressional Record* of the 37th Congress, this act granted 160 acres of public land in the West to "any person who is the head of a family, or who has arrived at the age of twenty-one years, and is a citizen of the United States, or who shall have filed his declaration of intention to become such." To receive his or her title to the homestead, the homesteader had to live on it for five years, build a home, and make certain other improvements.

Because free distribution of land in small parcels discouraged the spread of slavery, the homestead idea had long been opposed by the Southern states. Their secession cleared the way for its adoption. By 1900, about six hundred thousand farmers had received over eighty million acres of land through the Homestead Act. The act was not a complete success, though, because the best lands were quickly purchased by the railroads and land speculators, forcing settlers to buy from them rather than accepting free government lands which were much poorer in quality. Though it was modified several times, and the choice of free lands became extremely restricted, the Homestead Act remained in effect until 1977.

Speculators wait to enter the land office at Guthrie, Oklahoma, each hoping to obtain free land through the Homestead Act.

Many pioneers discovered when they reached their destination that good land near any river or lake was already owned—usually by a railroad company or a land speculator. Railroad companies, which owned far more land than they needed for their tracks and facilities, were notorious for land speculation. They had been given some land by the federal government, and the government allowed them first rights to purchase other land, as well. The railroad companies sold much of this land to settlers for 100 to 500 percent more than they had paid for it. Many settlers were forced to buy land from speculators rather than settle for free homestead lands that fell far short of their expectations.

The greatest shock to most pioneers was the scarcity of water in the West. Accustomed to the abundant rivers and lakes and relatively high rainfall levels of the eastern states, many pioneers did not think twice about the need for water until they arrived on their new farmland. The sight of the plains, covered with grass and wildflowers, rolling on for miles must have been breathtaking. But sooner or later, most of the new landowners began to wonder where the nearest river or lake was. Where was their water to come from? The answer, in most cases, was below the ground.

Water had to be pumped, and a well site had to be found right away. Thus, most settlers quickly became acquainted with one of their most prosperous neighbors: the driller. Using a divining rod and other highly unreliable techniques, the driller identified the spot where he believed the water to be nearest the surface. Then, harnessing his horse to a gear wheel that turned a large auger, he drilled into the ground. If he had not hit water by the time the top of the auger reached ground level, he started over in a new spot.

It might be days before the pioneer family secured a water supply. Once a reliable supply was found, a long cast-iron pipe was lowered into the freshly drilled hole, and a

A pioneer family crosses the Nebraska prairie in pursuit of a homestead. Pioneers fortunate enough to obtain land then faced the arduous task of locating an adequate water supply.

Once a pioneer family drilled a well and cleared the land for farming, they embarked on a new task—building a house. In heavily forested areas, pioneers had the resources to construct plain but sturdy log homes.

hand pump was attached at ground level. Then the family could begin to clear the land, prepare it for planting, and build a home. While the location of the water well usually determined the site for the house, the process of clearing the land provided materials.

The Sod House Frontier

In some cases, the land to be farmed was covered with forests, which supplied logs for a log home. On land where they planned to plant crops, the settlers cut down trees and uprooted the stumps. Then they stripped the bark from the logs, cut them to size, and carved notches in the corners, so that one log could be securely fastened atop another. They built the walls to a height of five or six feet and then cut doors and windows in the finished walls. To frame the roof, they split logs into lighter boards, over which they laid flat planks or tree boughs.

Most pioneers on the plains, however, owned land covered with prairie grass, which became the material they used to construct their houses. By 1865, sod houses dotted the prairies. Cut in rectangles about one foot thick, two feet wide, and three feet long, sod made extremely sturdy bricks. These units could be stacked much like clay bricks and held together by a mortar made of soft mud mixed with a little lye. Even the roof was made of sod bricks, which were usually covered by a layer of thatched grass and brush. An average "soddy," about sixteen feet by twenty feet, required about one acre of sod to build and, when finished, weighed nearly ninety tons.

The sod house protected its dwellers from heat and cold. In fact, it made a better insulator than either wood or brick. The dirt walls could even be made quite attractive when painted with a mixture of white clay and water. A Nebraska settler claimed that a sod house made an extremely comfortable

Life in the Rural North

home: "With doors and windows in place, with furniture brought from the old home . . . , with perhaps a carpet on the floor and an organ or piano and good furniture, a nice home could have been established."[60]

Facing Daily Hardships

The majority of settlers, however, could not afford to carpet a dirt floor. Nor could they afford good furniture, to say nothing of an organ or piano. The typical prairie pioneer family lived in a one-room sod house that leaked when it rained, almost always smelled musty, and lacked adequate ventilation. In wet weather, the walls and floor sweated, and in dry weather, they produced a constant supply of dust that covered everything—furniture, dishes, even food.

While magazines back East glamorized the life of the prairie pioneer and carried advertisements from land speculators picturing abundant rivers and forests, pioneers experienced something quite different. Farming "out West" was far more difficult and unpredictable than it was "back East." The winters on the plains were harsh, cold, and enduring. While spring brought relief from the cold, it also brought unpredictable, wildly fluctuating amounts of rainfall. All too often, much-needed rain was accompanied by unwanted thunder and lightning, hail, and even tornadoes. The weather often rendered the farmer's efforts useless, his crops destroyed by too little rainfall, or by hail.

A family sits in front of their elaborate sod home, located on the Nebraska plains. Ingenious pioneers discovered that prairie grass sod could be cut to form sturdy bricks useful in building.

A Native American chief forbids a wagon train to pass through his land. Tensions mounted between pioneers and Native Americans as immigrants continued to settle the West.

In addition, violent confrontations increased between the new settlers and the Native Americans who had roamed these prairies for centuries. The native tribes watched in silence as wagon trains carried a seemingly endless stream of settlers across their hunting grounds. Land thick with grass that had fed deer and buffalo was quickly transformed by these settlers into fields of wheat and corn. Some tribes waged violent attacks against the settlers.

Many pioneer families were defeated by the combination of backbreaking work, un-predictable conditions, and danger. They gave up their dreams of prosperity and returned to the predictable poverty of working in steel mills or textile plants, harboring a growing bitterness toward the "land of opportunity" and those who extended this promise. Yet slowly but surely, the Great Prairie was settled, and as church steeples and general stores dotted the horizon, pioneer settlers brought many of the same rural traditions to towns like Stevens Falls, Wisconsin; Dodge, Kansas; Omaha, Nebraska; and Bismarck, North Dakota.

6 Life in the Northern City

While the rural North was the stronghold of tradition, the cities of the North were cauldrons of change. Bursting at the seams with the arrival of immigrants and others seeking work in factories and shipyards, Northern cities reflected the changing face of America, both positively and negatively. New industries brought new opportunities and wealth to many. The factories, shipyards, and markets also drew floods of new workers to Northern cities, many of whom had emigrated from Europe. "A great melting pot," a phrase often used to describe America's mixture of ethnicities, originated during this period, and it aptly described most Northern cities.

Of the four million foreign-born people living in the United States in 1860, three million of them, and their American-born children, lived in Northern cities.

Most immigrant families arrived desperately poor, and they had already spent their life's savings for third-class passage on a steamer or a freighter from Europe to Boston or New York City. Of course, not all immigrants stepped off a ship and settled in New York and Boston. Many kept on going, to Detroit and Chicago, as well as to smaller manufacturing centers like Indianapolis and Cincinnati in the Midwest and Lynn and Lawrence, Massachusetts. Factory owners in these cities invited immigrant men, women, and even children to join the great industrial revolution that tripled American productivity and wealth between the years 1800 and 1860.

Skilled and unskilled workers alike were in great demand. The factories in Northern cities produced thousands of new jobs. Between 1820 and 1860, the urban popu-

Newly arrived Irish immigrants carry their belongings through the streets of New York City. The great influx of immigrants helped to boost the North's economy.

During the Civil War, over one million Americans lived in the bustling metropolis of New York City, shown here in 1860.

lation grew three times as fast as the rural population. In 1820 only 7 percent of all Americans lived in cities of over twenty-five hundred people. By 1860, this number had climbed to 20 percent.

Of course, the new economy did not reward all equally. A walk through New York, Chicago, or Cincinnati in 1862 would have provided the sojourner with a realistic cross section of America, from the elegant and stately homes of the successful entrepreneurs on the outskirts of the city to the row houses of the middle class—broadly defined to include lawyers, doctors, teachers, salespeople, and so on—and finally to the crowded, energetic, noisy, and squalid tenement districts of the working poor.

The "Country" Estate

A hike across New York City, already home to more than one million Americans, might begin on the outskirts of the city, where one would gain an impression of the luxury and prosperity enjoyed by the benefactors of the industrial revolution. Here were the older country estates, inhabited by families whose parents or grandparents had built the homes. Many of the residents took great pride in their "old money" and traditional ways, belonging to social groups like the Mayflower Society, whose members could all, supposedly, trace their ancestry back to the original Pilgrims who came over on the *Mayflower*.

The houses often reflected the owners' traditional roots and values. The most common country estate was built in the so-called Federal style, which dated back to the days of the American Revolution. Its rather unadorned, symmetrical, rectangular design reflected the practical, businesslike outlook of its owners. In its most elaborate form, the Federal-style house, all built of brick or brownstone, consisted of a central block two or three stories high flanked by conspicuously lower wings on either side.

By the 1850s, however, many wealthier Americans wanted their houses to set them apart, to display their wealth and their

Then, as now, Americans were in love with cars. In the Civil War era, of course, these cars were pulled by horses, but the make and style of the horse-drawn carriage was considered a significant statement about the owner's personality and status. From the New York Evening Post, August 23, 1864, here is a description of a highly customized barouche, the "Rolls-Royce" of carriages, including, of course, its "thorough-bred" horses and the attendants (footmen and postilions). Since the carriage was owned by a high official of the Democratic Party, the reporter has a little fun with the owner's "democratic" principles. To put the cost of this carriage in perspective, consider that a four-bedroom, two-story wood frame house could be purchased in 1864 for about $1,000.

"The equipage [rig] that throws all others in the shade, and causes them to 'pale their ineffectual fires,' is that of the . . . chairman of the Democratic National Committee. It consists of a low barouche drawn by four elegant and fiery "thorough-breds," with postilions mounted on the left or "near" horse of each pair. Two footmen in extreme [very fancy] livery are suspended from a high seat on the back of the carriage, technically called the 'rumble.' The barouche is lined with rich satin damask, and the outside trimmings are of heavy gilt. The postilions are dressed in buckskin breeches and high top boots, with black silk velvet jackets and caps highly ornamented with gold lace. The men are peculiarly well formed, having been selected and trained in Europe with especial reference to their 'build' and the extra size of their 'calves.' Their livery is imported at a cost of about $1,000 a suit, and the cost of the whole affair may be conjectured [estimated] when I state that the horses are valued at $25,000, the carriage at $5,000, and the harness and other trappings at $3,000. When the royal cortege [procession] makes its appearance on the avenue with the democratic prince in full costume, all other vehicles instinctively give way, as though the occupant was indeed a 'crowned head' [foreign ruler]. The stables of his democratic majesty are said to contain some forty horses."

individuality. They asked architects to design homes that were not only a retreat from the business world, but a flight into the grandeur of the past—especially the European past. Inspired by romantic poets and writers like Washington Irving, these architects revived the more ornate European styles known as the Gothic. For this reason, many of the large country homes designed around the time of the Civil War are called Gothic Revival homes. Ornately designed and decorated, these houses varied widely in style. In fact, Andrew Jackson Downing, author and architect, summarized the Gothic Revival philoso-phy in his 1850 book, *The Architecture of Country Houses*, by emphasizing variety:

A blind partiality for any one style in building is detrimental to the progress of improvement. A wide vocabulary of historic motifs adds novelty to architecture, creates variety, and bestows symbolic associations.

The lover of art and landscape can have a dwelling in the Tuscan style; the wealthy landowner, a castellated home; the leisured gentleman, a Tudor residence;

the man of modest means and good taste, a dwelling in the bracketed style. A Swiss cottage in the Hudson or Allegheny Highlands; a Gothic dwelling in New England. In the middle states the Romanesque or Norman style . . . in the West the manners of an Italian villa. For the artisan, a cottage; for the merchant, a villa; for the gentleman, a mansion.[61]

The Urban Mansion

Many leaders of the new industrial movement found that they needed to live in the city, near their business interests and close to banks and other investors. Yet they did not want to forfeit the sense of quiet luxury that came with a country estate. Therefore, they built mansions on large city estates and surrounded their houses with beautiful gardens, sprawling lawns, and shade trees. To this day, a number of these urban mansions, such as the Astor Home in New York City, the Brown House, built by the founder of Brown University in Providence, Rhode Island, and Blair House, once the Washington, D.C.,

home of President Lincoln's postmaster general, Montgomery Blair, are still in use.

The enormous Blair House, which occupies an entire city block, is used today to house official guests of the federal government. During the Civil War, Montgomery Blair was one of Lincoln's most trusted advisers, and the president often made the short walk from the White House to Blair House. In a small room to the right of the front entrance, just a few days after becoming president, Abraham Lincoln interviewed Colonel Robert E. Lee and offered him the command of the Union army, which Lee, of course, declined.

Modern Services Begin in the North

As Northern cities grew, they began to organize and expand their services. Prior to the Civil War, law enforcement in most cities was in the hands of an elected sheriff or constable, who deputized local volunteers whenever he saw the need. Uniformed police forces, organized by the city and paid with

Police forces in New York City (pictured) and other Northern cities began wearing uniforms and receiving pay from the city during the Civil War years.

A doctor dispenses medicine to an ill patient during a house call. Many doctors who practiced medicine during the 1800s received little or no medical schooling and instead gained their experience by apprenticing with a well-known physician.

city taxes, first began to appear around the time of the Civil War. After serving in the war, many retired officers took up police work. Cities also began to employ full-time firefighters, and in 1865 the U.S. Post Office began to offer free door-to-door mail delivery in cities of over fifty thousand people. Thus an entirely new class of semiprofessionals arose, the civil servants. Besides policemen and firefighters, civil servants included letter carriers, post office clerks, court clerks, schoolteachers, and park supervisors. This new class of semiprofessionals and the traditional professionals, like doctors, lawyers, and clergymen, usually lived in middle-class neighborhoods.

The Respectable Profession of Medicine

The most respected professional people in town were the clergymen, lawyers, bankers, and, above all, the doctors. However, the respect accorded to the local physician usual-

ly had little to do with his training. Until the mid-1870s, course work at the nation's 110 medical schools remained ridiculously easy. Few medical schools required more than a high school diploma for entrance, and some asked only for the ability to read and write English. The course work at the typical medical school could be completed in a year or less, and few schools offered any laboratory work or required their students to intern under an experienced doctor. States had no licensing or exam procedure to ensure the competence of practicing physicians.

Some physicians practiced without ever having set foot inside a medical school. They received their training through apprenticeships, working as a physician's assistant, in addition to handling his accounts, chopping wood, sweeping his office, and running errands. The apprentice often harnessed his master's horse and buggy and drove him to house calls, where he observed how to lance boils, set fractures, amputate limbs, and administer a "bleeding," which was the preferred treatment for fever. After a three-year apprenticeship, the assistant was ready to strike out on his own.

One young physician looking for a place to set up his practice received a letter from a town in western Illinois. The town already had five doctors, but it seemed that they were all Republicans, while the majority of the townsfolk were Democrats. "If you come here, you can commence all the democratic practice besides some of the other," promised the recruiter. "I can insure your introduction into many of the best families here. . . . You will find a set of public men here that will do what they can for you."[62]

Middle-Class Lifestyles

The middle-class family that could afford to own a home typically had a row house. Row houses, many of which still stand in our eastern cities, were incredibly narrow, two- or three-story homes built side by side. In fact, adjacent row houses usually shared a common wall. Because they were so long and narrow, most row houses were similar in overall design. Upon entering, one would typically face a wooden stairway and a long, narrow hallway. Off this hallway, and behind the stairway, the ground floor contained a parlor, a dining room, and a kitchen, and, sometimes, a second parlor. Up the flight of stairs, one would normally find a similar arrangement, except that the rooms off the hallway were bedrooms.

Boarding and Renting

Men and young couples without children often chose to board. The boardinghouse was usually owned by a widow or by a couple whose family had left home. Bedrooms were available, usually on a weekly basis, and the rent covered the cost of meals as well. Boarders did not have to worry about furnishing their quarters or about buying and preparing food. All the boarders at a single house shared a common table and a common parlor.

Many Americans preferred boarding to renting an apartment, which would require the acquisition of furniture. The middle-class apartment, a relatively new concept in the 1860s, had originated in France. The first middle-class apartment buildings in this country appeared in New Orleans, and many Northerners referred to them by the rather derogatory term "French flats." As the decade moved on, however, apartment living became increasingly popular. Renting an apartment

Middle-class urban families often lived in row houses. These tall and narrow houses usually shared a common wall with their neighbors and were nearly identical in design.

was usually cheaper than paying room and board at a boardinghouse, and it afforded the renter far greater privacy.

Shopping in the City

One reason for living in the city in this era before automobiles was the ability to take advantage of urban shopping and entertainment opportunities. The experience of shopping began to change dramatically during the Civil War era. The nation's first department store, A. T. Stewart's, opened on Broadway in New York City in 1862. The department store, the urban version of the country general store, carried nearly as wide a variety of dry goods, but no food. No one would mistake the cozy, cluttered general store, though, for the spacious, luxurious department store, which began the same transition in merchandising that had already taken place in manufacturing. The small, privately operated shop, in which the owner and his family waited on customers personally, gave way to the large, corporate-owned store, in which the customers were served by clerks (usually young women) and cashiers (usually men).

When A. T. Stewart's first opened in New York City, it introduced a new kind of glamour and elegance to shopping. It was an immediate hit. When visitors came to the city, the first thing most of them wanted to see was A. T. Stewart's. The five-story building, occupying an entire block on Broadway, gave New Yorkers a glimpse of the future. It featured cast-iron facades, rows of plate-glass display windows, and hydraulic passenger elevators. Inside, a mammoth rotunda extending from the ground floor to a domed ceiling above the fifth floor gave Stewart's a sense of grandeur unmatched by many cathedrals. Departments on the four upper floors encircled the rotunda, allowing patrons to peer over the iron railings at the hubbub below. In the basement, eight enormous boilers drove ten steam engines, which provided power for three elevators, gave steam heat in

Northern women browse in the lace department of the luxurious A. T. Stewart's. This modern department store offered its customers both glamour and elegance and catered to their every whim.

Early "Billboards"

Since the time of the industrial revolution (and perhaps even earlier), Americans have led the world in developing marketing techniques. Travelers in the New England countryside encountered big advertisements painted on boulders alongside the roadways. An English tourist in New Hampshire, quoted in Smith and Judah's Life in the North During the Civil War, *was not impressed with these forerunners of the modern billboard advertisement.*

"The whole of this beautiful district is very curiously disfigured by the manner in which the rocks are covered with advertisements. The great advertisers in America scorn to confine themselves to newspapers—they stamp their advertisements on the face of nature; so that not only he who runs may read, but must read whether he likes or not. Every prominent rock, not only in the White Mountain district but along the beautiful banks of the Hudson and in every place where travelers must congregate, is carefully painted in large letters with the name of some specific or other—the most persistently obtrusive being the 'plantation bitters,' and 'sozodont,' a preparation for the teeth. If you stand by the Profile Mountain to gaze on the wonderful old stone face, you eye is arrested by 'Drake's Plantation Bitter,'—if you pause by Echo Lake to listen, you are met by invitations to 'Try the Sozodont.'. . . 'O, don't,' wrote a wag underneath."

winter, and kept hot water flowing to the fifth-floor laundry.

Stewart's employed about two thousand people, over half of them women. While most women labored as seamstresses, laundresses, and janitors, and men dominated the managerial and cashier positions, a growing number of women worked as salesclerks. Since the store placed a heavy emphasis on women's clothing and household goods, it made sense for women clerks to wait on the predominantly female clientele. The actual money handling, however, was still done almost exclusively by men.

Unlike its country cousin the general store, the department store emphasized courtesy and elegance. Open from 7 A.M. to 7 P.M., Stewart's doors were tended by door boys, who also offered to take charge of customers' umbrellas. Male ushers, scattered throughout the store, directed customers to the department they sought, where over three hundred eager salesmen and -women stood waiting to serve them. After making a sale, a salesperson summoned a "cash boy" to carry the payment and invoice to one of the cashiers, who collected the money and sent the cash boy back to the customer with a receipt and any change due. Each department store cashier sat in a little wooden booth enclosed with lattice work.

Though these big stores weakened the traditional tie between customer and owner, they gave new opportunities to many men and women to enter the retail business. Of course, it took another forty or fifty years for this trend to reach New England villages and midwestern towns. There the general store remained the focal point of community activity through the end of the century, when department store chains, like Sears, began to appear in their territory.

This 1875 photo captures a quiet day on Broadway in New York City. The enormous A. T. Stewart's is visible on the right, occupying an entire city block.

The Fashion-Conscious Middle Class

Not by chance, the popularity of the department store coincided with the rapid rise in subscriptions to newspapers and magazines. Together, these media introduced a much broader segment of the American population than ever before to commercialism. As a result, millions of middle-class Americans became fashion conscious. Magazines and newspapers carried ads for men's and ladies' clothing, accessories, and toiletries. The fascination expressed by one young gentleman with his new bride's morning routine sounds strikingly modern:

> Her daintily draped dressing table is piled high with pots of face creams, boxes of powder, and rouge. She spent long hours applying ice packs to her lovely throat and bosom and brushed to lac-

quered brightness her black hair, and even did calisthenics each morning.[63]

Although the use of rouge, eye shadow, and other cosmetics increased dramatically during the 1860s, many people still clung to their "old-fashioned ways." They looked on all this makeup as a sure sign that young women of the 1860s were becoming immoral. One gentleman issued this warning to ladies who dared to use such products: "If women, prompted by no other motive than that of pleasing men, paint their faces, I solemnly declare to them, in the name of the masculine sex, that they are going a false route and will only render themselves horrible."[64]

Local Entertainment

People who lived in the city were able to take advantage of the art and entertainment venues that the city offered. America's love affair with the stage began in the 1800s, as New England Puritan disapproval of theater gradually weakened. Enterprising businessmen in New York, Boston, and other cities built theaters to host a wide variety of public amusements. New York became the center of American theater, and Edwin Booth's magnificent Renaissance-style theater on Sixth Avenue was generally acknowledged as the nation's finest. Theater fare during the Civil War era included not only opera, serious drama, and melodrama, but burlesque, vaudeville, and minstrel shows, featuring singing,

Popular Northern magazines and newspapers introduced millions of Americans to new fashions. As a result, the middle class grew increasingly fashion conscious.

dancing, comedy, and an abundance of scantily clad women performing the "can-can." New England preachers were beside themselves; organizations of churchwomen condemned the young temptresses who "display everything but self respect"; and men's opera glasses sold like hotcakes.

Sports and Recreation in Northern Cities

As the cities became increasingly industrial, their skylines began to sprout smokestacks and tenement apartment buildings. To preserve some greenery and open space, civic leaders urged municipalities to buy huge parcels of land to serve as city parks. The land for the nation's largest city park, Central Park in New York City, was purchased by that city in 1856.

As city parks emerged, they had a profound effect on sports and recreation in the North. Before the 1850s, recreation had been exclusively an individual or family affair. There were no organized sports teams and no professional sports at all, unless one counts prizefighting, which, although extremely popular, was carried out secretly in local saloons. The traditional Puritan influence still led most respected citizens to discourage, at least in public, the watching of prizefights or any other contest as a degrading waste of valuable time.

Watching prizefights and gambling on them remained popular, but by 1850 another sport, baseball, had stolen the hearts of many Americans. At first, local baseball teams were strictly amateur, but baseball fields with bleachers began to appear in city parks, and many townsfolk enjoyed gathering on Saturday afternoons to watch the young men of one town or neighborhood take on those from another town or neighborhood.

The nation's most celebrated theater was built by renowned actor Edwin Booth. At Booth's Theater, patrons were entertained by a wide array of performances, ranging from operas to burlesque shows.

The National Association of Base Ball Players, the first baseball league in America, was established in 1857. An organization of 25 amateur teams, all in cities east of the Mississippi, the association formalized a schedule of games and drew up rules for deciding a national championship. Baseball received a tremendous boost from the Civil War, when many soldiers traveling to eastern cities became exposed to the game. Upon returning home, these veterans formed teams in their cities and towns. By

"Blood and Thunder" Dramas

Opera and serious drama were available in New York and other major cities, but most Americans favored sensational melodramas and slapstick comedies, which were produced by traveling companies or local amateurs in small local theaters, or "opera houses." Nearly every town had at least one. The most popular showplace for such "blood and thunder" drama was the Bowery Theater in New York City. The melodramas, featuring sizzling plots of death and destruction, differed little from one another. Each included a panorama of swooning heroines, courageous heroes, wicked villains, flirtatious saloon girls, and comic buffoons.

Audiences at theaters like the Bowery could be as fascinating as the plays. "Every nook and cranny is occupied," recounted one witness. "The suckling infant. . . . The youngster rubbing his sleepy eyes. The timid Miss, half frightened with the great mob and longing for the fairy world to be created. Elder boys and elder sisters. Mothers, fathers, and the wrinkled old grandsire." Add a few sailors, some shop girls, clerks, and tradesmen, and the audience provided a pretty good cross section of the lower middle class and the working class.

The audiences were not bashful about joining in the action either. They cheered when the hero rescued his sweetheart from the jaws of death; they hissed when the mustache-twirling villain slunk onto the stage. Wandering through this animated audience were red-shirted peanut vendors. "Almost every jaw in the vast concern is crushing nut-shells," complained one patron. "You fancy you can hear it in the lulls of the play like a low unbroken growl."

1866, the National Association had grown to 202 teams.

The game itself was played a little differently in the nineteenth century. A bat and a ball were the only pieces of equipment in use. The ball was caught barehanded by all players, including the catcher, who did not wear a protective mask. Fortunately, the ball was larger, softer, and bouncier than today's baseball. It did not hurt as much to be struck by such a ball, but catching it was also less predictable. Consequently, professional scores like 103 to 80 were not uncommon! Umpires had only minimal control of the game, and often, after making a particularly unpopular call, they had to run for their lives to avoid being mobbed by players and fans alike.

But it was in the empty fields and open lots, where boys swung bats made from shovel handles and tossed balls that were wads of rags held together with homemade paste, that baseball became the national pastime. A tree, a stream, or a nearby warehouse marked the home run boundary, while flat stones served as bases. In May 1867, an Algona, Iowa, newspaper announced that anyone interested in forming a local league for boys should meet at the town square on Saturday afternoons. Within weeks, the boys and their parents had laid out a diamond and begun playing games every Wednesday and Saturday afternoon during the summer.

The North's Working Poor

More than half the Northern population fell into the relatively prosperous upper or middle class, but that still left a large portion unaccounted for: the working poor. Many poor people had come to the cities, either from across the Atlantic, or from family homes in the country, seeking prosperity.

Prizefighting: America's First Professional Sport

Before professional baseball was born, men were paid to participate in the sport of prizefighting. Since most of the money for purses, or sums awarded to winners, was raised through gambling, the prizefight was illegal in most cities and had to be conducted "in secret." The secret was poorly guarded, though, as the fight, or slate of fights, usually took place in a local saloon before hundreds of raucous, screaming spectators.

Prizefighting—one could hardly call it boxing—was a brutal, bare-knuckles, murderous form of entertainment with few rules and no scoring system. A fight usually lasted until one of the opponents was knocked unconscious or gave up. Quite often, the victor would continue to take on challengers from the crowd, and the fights would continue late into the night. A reporter in Virginia City, Nevada, described the action at a local saloon:

> I stopped to see a regular knock down in a crib . . . called P. McCarthy's Saloon. The doors were fastened, but I got a chance to peek in the window— [the contestants] were stripped to their drawers and had fought several rounds already. . . . They were bloody as butchers—both badly punished.

They had not found it, however, despite their determination and energy.

Although most had not abandoned the hope of working their way out of poverty, they lived in dismal tenements, usually abandoned warehouses or row houses that had been divided into minuscule two- or three-room apartments. Typically a family of five lived in a tenement apartment that

Not long after its introduction, baseball became the national pastime. On October 22, 1866, the Philadelphia Athletics and the Brooklyn Atlantics vied for the national championship (pictured) before crowds of cheering spectators.

consisted of a ten-foot by twelve-foot living room and one "bedroom" that was not even big enough to hold a double bed. The tenements lacked water and gas, and usually relied on wood- or coal-burning cookstoves to heat individual apartments. Seldom did a tenement apartment contain more than a single window.

The scarcity of windows was perhaps not a serious disadvantage, since the tenement districts were so filthy and overcrowded that there was little fresh air to be had. In New York City, like most American cities, street cleaning, garbage collection, and sewage disposal were provided only to citizens who paid for the services. Most of the working poor who lived in tenement houses could not afford

these fees, so garbage of all kinds—dead animals, factory waste, sewage, and spoiled food—piled up in the streets. One New York reporter described the conditions in Five Points, a rugged district in New York City:

> The population is dense and as little addicted to cleanliness as godliness. The streets . . . are generally matted with the foulest garbage, thrown from the houses in defiance of law and decency. . . . In winter, huge heaps of ashes are added to the piles of kitchen and grocer garbage, both intermingled with fouler filth.[65]

The filthy conditions of the tenements bred smallpox, typhus, and other illnesses.

Twelve thousand cases of typhoid fever were reported in New York in one year. In the same city, in the single month of August 1864, seventeen hundred infants died from disease. In Washington, crowded to the bursting point during the war, an outbreak of smallpox killed thousands, many of them black refugees living in squalid camps on the outskirts of the city. The disease spread as slum dwellers sold the clothes of the dead to secondhand dealers; no one at the time realized that this practice was an ideal way of transmitting a highly contagious disease.

Work Conditions of the Lower Class

The majority of Northerners who lived in impoverished conditions were immigrants, many of whom had come to America hoping to earn enough to buy a piece of land and the equipment to farm it. Others hoped to run their own businesses. For some, the dream came true; but for most, life took on a dreary sameness, day after day, month after month, and year after year. Six days a week, ten or more hours a day, they worked at monotonous

Cincinnati Red Stockings: The First Professional Baseball Team

Although the National Association of Base Ball Players was an organization of amateurs, it provided the soil from which the roots of professional sports soon began to sprout. In 1867, a Chicago team paid Albert G. Spalding, the future sporting goods manufacturer, $40 a week, ostensibly to be a wholesale grocery clerk, but really to be their pitcher. In 1869 the Cincinnati Red Stockings ended the charade and paid baseball players direct salaries, ranging from $800 to $1,400 a season, which was a very handsome wage in those days. When the Red Stockings defeated every team they faced that summer, trouncing one hapless opponent 103 to 8, the advantages of professionalism became apparent. Soon, baseball organizations all over the country were offering money to players— usually a fixed amount per game—and charging admission of spectators. The National Association opposed the trend toward professional athletics, but the floodgates had already opened. The National League of Professional Baseball Clubs was established in 1870.

In 1869, the Cincinnati Red Stockings became America's first professional baseball team.

and exhausting jobs in steel mills, shoe and textile factories, or munitions plants. What they earned was barely enough to buy food and pay rent for the family.

A number of immigrants had been domestic servants in Europe, where they had little or no hope of ever rising beyond that class. In the United States, they found factory jobs at which they toiled sixty or more hours a week. Those with families to support, however, managed to save little, if any, of their earnings. In the end, many returned to domestic service. They gave up their dreams of financial independence for the consolation of a comfortable place to live.

Others resorted to a deceptively simple labor arrangement known as tenement living: a manufacturer bought a block of tenements and rented the apartments to unskilled laborers, to whom he also supplied sewing machines, cigar-rolling apparatus, or other materials to make a desired product. Laborers paid their rent to the manufacturer by producing a specified quantity, receiving a few cents extra for each item produced beyond the quota. The tenement system encouraged couples and families to work long hours to get ahead. Some families managed to save enough to break out of poverty; many, however, were victimized by unscrupulous landlords who continually raised their rents, preventing them from doing anything but working harder.

Child Labor Practices

One of the most hopeful developments in the North was free public education, available in every Northern state to all children, at least theoretically. For children whose parents had

The North's working poor lived in run-down and overcrowded tenements or apartment buildings that were located in slum districts.

Families living in tenements were forced to put all of their children to work if they hoped to both pay their rent and save some money.

the wisdom and will to send them, education was the best road away from the dead end of poverty. It prepared young men to enter a business, go into banking, or attend college to study law, medicine, or another profession. Many young women studied to be teachers, which in some states required only a high school diploma. Less than half of all poor children, however, attended public schools. Some parents, especially Catholic immigrants, feared that the public school would indoctrinate their children with Protestant beliefs and turn them against their heritage. For others, it was a practical decision. They did not send their children to public school because they could not do without the income the children could earn by holding full-time jobs.

Hundreds of thousands of children, some as young as six years old, worked alongside their parents in factories, mines, and shops. In 1860, the federal government estimated that 110,000 children worked as domestic servants, and another hundred thousand worked in factories or mines. This estimate was undoubtedly low, however, because most employers did not report employees *under* ten years old! Apparently ten was considered a reasonable age for children to start working. Also, to earn anything beyond their monthly rent, families trapped in tenement setups usually had to have all the children—even four- and five-year-olds—working.

The children who worked in factories were usually expected to do the same jobs as the adults, and for just as many hours. Nevertheless, most manufacturers paid younger workers less, arguing that they did not produce as much as full-grown employees. A *New York Herald* article written in 1863 reported the following conversation between a woman of the wealthy class and a ten-year-old orphan girl who worked in a factory stripping feathers:

> "What kind of work is stripping feathers?" one woman asked a fatherless ten-year-old working girl.
>
> "Why, like that in your hat," she responded. "That is what they are like when we have finished them; but we girls work at them before they are dyed. I make about three dollars a week, and my sister—she is only six years old—she does not make as much; sometimes a dollar a week, sometimes more."[66]

Children who worked in factories also faced the same dangers as their adult coworkers. The most common injuries to factory children occurred in twine or yarn factories, in which a girl (mostly girls worked in these factories) could easily lose a finger in a "twister machine." One owner of such a factory admitted that his factory girls were occasionally injured if they were not careful, but he refused to accept any responsibility for the accidents: "A few girls have had their fingers hurt in these machines; but it is always in cases where they forgot or neglected their work to talk or play. The twisters are not more dangerous than other machines at which children work."[67]

Other boys and girls worked as street vendors, selling newspapers, matches, tobacco, fruits, candy, balloons, dogs, cats, birds—anything and everything. Of course, the children on the streets were not their own bosses. Men trying to scratch out a living supplied the children with wares and took most of the money from their sales. These men all hoped that someday they would save enough to move from being street vendors to achieve the status of shop owner. Only a handful ever made it.

A young street vendor walks the streets hawking newspapers. During the nineteenth century, children as young as ten years of age could legally work alongside adults in factories and at other jobs.

New Tensions Emerge

Life in the tenements was difficult, and it could be dreary, but here one also encountered the robust energy of the working class, the people who actually provided the power that drove the great economic engine of the North. One would find the unique sounds, colors, and rhythms of Irish neighborhoods, Italian neighborhoods, and German neighborhoods, as most people tended to seek the comfort of familiar languages and customs.

The ambition of most working-class people in these neighborhoods, though, was to get away from them. Understandably, determination often turned to tension and frustration. For one thing, many of the working poor began to believe that they were carrying the greatest burden of the war while wealthy investors profited. True, many prominent Northern men joined the Union army, especially at first; but most of them joined as generals or colonels, at which rank, army life was both more comfortable and less dangerous than for the average enlisted man. As the war progressed, the percentage of well-to-do enlistees declined, and when the draft went into effect, a great number of wealthy Northerners whose names were drawn paid their $300 commutation fee to have someone else take their place. For many working-class Americans, the Civil War brought much of this simmering tension to the boiling point.

Racial and Political Tensions

In all ages, societies are pulled in opposite directions by the desire to maintain traditions and the need to accommodate change and innovation, but the tension between these forces was perhaps more dramatic during the Civil War era than at any other time in American history, before or since. Certainly the war between the states and the threat to national union intensified Americans' feelings and drove them to identify with one group or another. However, the war itself was a product of economic and social shifts that had changed the economy, the work, and the lifestyles of Americans. In the North, where these shifts occurred more rapidly than in the South, the changes were both welcomed and feared. They brought new opportunities to some, but they also threatened old securities, created new classes of poor, and introduced new divisions among the people of the North.

A great deal of the tension and resentment among the people in the working class became aimed in the direction of the newest members of the working poor, the former slaves who had fled the South by the thousands after emancipation. Unskilled, uneducated, knowing no life except that of a slave on a Southern

After emancipation, thousands of former slaves migrated to the North. Many Northerners feared the new immigrants would disrupt their economy and lifestyle.

The signing of the Emancipation Proclamation. President Lincoln issued the historic document giving freedom to slaves on September 22, 1862.

plantation, many members of this group found great difficulty adjusting to a new life in the North. The experience was not made any easier by the prejudice and resentment they encountered. Many in the Northern white population, feeling economic and social pressures from several directions, lashed out at the easiest and most defenseless target they could find: black people in general.

The Emancipation Controversy

At the outset of the Civil War, 220,000 free blacks were living in the Northern states. Although President Lincoln believed that slavery should eventually be abolished throughout the nation, for the first year of the Civil War, he rarely mentioned the issue. Not until the summer of 1862, when it became

evident that emancipating the Southern slaves could strike the South a knockout blow, did Lincoln begin to seriously consider this policy option. By the summer, he had become convinced that declaring all slaves in the South free would create havoc in the South and help carry the North to victory. On September 22, 1862, therefore, Abraham Lincoln issued the Emancipation Proclamation. As of January 1, 1863, the proclamation announced, all slaves in states still in rebellion would be "thenceforth and forever free."

During the first eighteen months of the war, Lincoln resisted this action, despite the urging of several members of his cabinet. The president knew that citizens disagreed bitterly over the issue of emancipation, and he did not want anything to divert them from the goal of restoring the Union. Although Lincoln opposed slavery, he considered the

Feeling the Pinch

While farmers, business owners, and investors thrived in the booming economy, only a small number passed this benefit on to their employees. For the working poor, making ends meet became tougher because of inflation. A July 4, 1863, article in Fincher's Trades Review, *excerpted by Smith and Judah in* Life in the North During the Civil War, *shows the drastic inflation in the prices of staples from 1861, when the war began, to 1863. Notice the dramatic rise in "muslins," or cotton products, and also coffee and tea, which, before the war, came to the North by way of Southern ports.*

"Two years ago, the man who received $1.50 per day, could satisfy his wants with that sum just as well, if not better, than he can now with $3.00 per day. Nearly every article of consumption has doubled, and if wages are not permitted to keep pace with the cost of necessaries, the producer is daily robbed of one half his earnings. Let us look at [the following figures;] . . . the difference we submit between that time and the present, can be verified by every housewife:

	1861	1863
Beef	$.08 to .10/lb.	$.15 to .18/lb.
Lamb	$.08 to .10/lb.	$.14 to .23/lb.
Mutton	$.06 to .08/lb.	$.13 to .15/lb.
Coffee	$.10 to .16/lb.	$.30 to .50/lb.
Tea	$.35 to 1.00/lb.	$1.00 to 2.50/lb.
Sugar	$.05 to .10/lb.	$.12 to .20/lb.
Rice	$.04 to .05/lb.	$.10 to .12/lb.
Muslins	$.06 to .12/lb.	$.25 to .50/lb."

secession of the Southern states too high a price to pay for its abolition. He made it clear that this war was being fought to preserve the United States as one nation, not to free the slaves. In August 1862, the president discussed his views in an open letter to Horace Greeley, editor of the *New York Tribune*:

My paramount objective in this struggle is to save the Union, and is not either to save or to destroy slavery. If I could save the Union without freeing any slave, I would do it, and if I could save it by freeing all the slaves, I would do it; and if I could save it by freeing some and leaving others alone, I would also do that.[68]

Among those urging Lincoln to do away with slavery in the South were the abolitionists, who argued not only that slavery was immoral but that any practice of inequality made a mockery of the principles of freedom and democracy. The abolitionist movement was represented by many of the North's best-known intellectuals—William Lloyd Garrison, Frederick Douglass, Salmon P. Chase, Harriet Beecher Stowe, Ralph Waldo Emerson, and numerous others—and, while they made up only a small percentage of the population, they were very articulate and influential.

Northern Reaction to the Emancipation Proclamation

Although reaction in the North was mixed, the majority of Northerners opposed the proclamation. In congressional and local elections of 1862, Democrats had exploited popular fears and hostility against blacks to win back some of the legislative seats they had lost in 1860. Some Union soldiers declared that they had no interest in dying to free slaves. Shortly before the Emancipation Proclamation took effect, one soldier wrote home to his fiancée:

It is not for the emancipation of the African race I fight. I want nothing to do with the negro. I want them as far from me as is possible to conceive. . . . When President Lincoln declares the slaves emancipated, I will declare myself no longer an American citizen.[69]

Emancipation drew violent reactions from some quarters. Residents of Irish sections in several cities became notorious for their violent treatment of any black person who happened to be found in the neighborhood. A reporter for the *Christian Recorder*, a newspaper in Philadelphia, reported that "Even here, . . . in many places it is almost impossible for a respectable colored person to walk the streets without being insulted by a set of blackguards and cowards."[70]

Much of the tension and division arose in the slums, or tenement neighborhoods, of Northern cities, where the families of unskilled, poorly paid workers—mostly European immigrants—lived. During the first two years or so of the war, they did little more than grumble, but as the war continued, members of the poor working class began to feel that most of the burdens of the war were being placed on their shoulders. In many ways, their feelings were justified. As the wartime economy soared, so did prices; but the wages of the factory and tenement workers still hovered at the bare subsistence level.

Many immigrant families forced themselves to live as frugally as possible so that they could save a little bit of money each month, but as their rents rose and the prices of food and clothing climbed, they found themselves sinking deeper into debt just to feed themselves and their children.

Two events of the latter half of the Civil War—emancipation and conscription—

seemed to reinforce the growing discouragement of the working poor. While most supporters of emancipation came from the ranks of the more prosperous, better-educated, predominantly Protestant upper class, the day-to-day effects of emancipation were experienced by the less prosperous, less educated, predominantly Catholic immigrants. Thus to the working poor, the Emancipation Proclamation and the new policy of conscription smacked of hypocrisy.

As thousands of blacks moved North, it was the already overcrowded tenement districts that received them, not the spacious suburbs or even the middle-class neighborhoods. Similarly, when wartime inflation shrunk the buying power of workers' wages, and their hopes of escaping poverty shrank as

An angry Northerner tries to expel a black gentleman from a "whites only" railroad car. The North's black population suffered from prejudice and violence committed by whites.

well, they blamed their low pay on blacks, many of whom were willing to work even more cheaply.

Although the resentment of the working poor usually led to unfounded bigotry and hatred toward blacks, their frustration can be understood. Moreover, blacks constituted the only group they could realistically attack. The Emancipation Proclamation, issued in 1862, heated up the frustration of many poor whites; and the Conscription Act of 1863 brought that frustration to a boil.

Draft Riots

By 1863, what had begun as a great flood of volunteers for the Union army had slowed to a trickle. This drop-off in troop strength prompted Congress to enact the Conscription Act, making it legal for the army to draft American citizens. Because of the $300 commutation option, the weight of the draft came to rest most heavily on the shoulders of poor white Americans. Unsurprisingly, the Union army became more and more a poor man's army, as wealthy draftees paid their way out and needy volunteers accepted bonuses to join.

A growing number of Northerners began to complain that this war was being fought by the poor, while the rich sold arms and supplies at a profit to the government. Democratic politicians and journalists fanned the flames of resentment against the Republican-led Congress that had voted for both emancipation and conscription. Strident editorials claimed that poor white men were being

At this New York recruiting station, a blindfolded official draws names for the draft. Dwindling numbers of volunteers forced the Union to enact the Conscription Act of 1863, which allowed the army to draft U.S. citizens.

Life in the North During the Civil War

forced into service and driven to their deaths in a war to free Negroes, who would ultimately come North and take jobs away from poor white men.

These ideas led to a series of so-called draft riots in cities across the North. Among the least popular citizens in any town or city were the conscription officers, whose duty it was to serve draft papers on those whose names had been drawn. In many cities, rowdy mobs gathered at local recruiting stations or other military offices to protest the draft. The protests often got out of hand and led to violent confrontations between civilians and the soldiers on duty.

The most notorious episodes were the New York draft riots of July 1863. An article in the *New York Times*, dated July 14, 1863, describes how the riots began in front of the army provost-marshal's office in downtown New York City and eventually raged out of control:

> As early as 9:00, some laborers employed by two or three railroad companies, and in the iron foundries on the eastern side of the city, formed in procession in the Twenty-second Ward, and visited the different workshops in the upper wards, where large numbers were employed, and compelled them, by threats in some instances, to cease their work. As the crowd [grew], their shouts and disorderly demonstrations became more formidable. . . . Scarcely had two dozen names been called [by the drafting officers], when a crowd, numbering perhaps 500, suddenly made an irruption in front of the building, attacking it with clubs, stones, bricks, and other missiles. . . . Following these missiles, the mob rushed furiously into the office on the first floor, where the draft was going on, seizing the

The Fear of "Africanization"

In a speech delivered to Congress in June 1862, Democratic representative Samuel Sullivan Cox of Ohio predicted that if Southern slaves were emancipated, Ohio would be "Africanized." Cox's speech, an excerpt of which is given here, can be found in the Congressional Record *for the 37th Congress. It demonstrates how the attitudes of many Northerners were built on prejudice and hearsay rather than on reasonable evidence.*

"Our soldiers, when they return, one hundred thousand strong, to their Ohio homes, will find these negroes, . . . filling their places, felling timber, plowing ground, gathering crops, &c. Labor that now ranges from one to two dollars per day, will fall to one half. . . . Nor is the labor of most of these negroes desirable. . . . They will get their week's wages, and then idle the week away. . . . If they are distributed into the country, they may work for a little time and for small wages, and work well for a time; but when work grows irksome, and they become too lazy to work, they will steal. Corn and chickens are known to disappear in their vicinage [vicinity]."

books, papers, records, lists, &c, all of which they destroyed. . . . The drafting officers were set upon with stones and clubs, and, with the reporters for the Press and others, had to make a hasty exit through the rear.

A small company of Union soldiers assigned to a local army hospital was sent to quell the riot, and this is what happened next:

Union soldiers fire on rioters during the New York draft riots of July 1863. Riots erupted throughout the North following the enactment of the Conscription Act.

Facing the rioters, the [soldiers] were ordered to fire, which many of them did, the shots being blank cartridges, but the smoke had scarce cleared away when the company (which did not number more than fifty men, if as many) were attacked and completely demoralized by the mob, who were armed with clubs, sticks, swords, and other implements. The soldiers had their bayonets taken away, and they themselves were compelled to seek refuge in the side streets, but in attempting to flee thither, several, it is said, were killed, while those that escaped, did so only to be hunted like dogs. . . . They were chased by the mob, who divided themselves into squads, and frequently a single soldier would be caught in a side street . . . and the poor fellow would be beaten almost to death.

Elated with success, the mob, which by this time had been largely reinforced, next formed themselves into marauding parties, and paraded through the neighboring streets, looking more like so many infuriated demons, the men being more or less intoxicated, dirty and half clothed. . . . The streets were thronged with women and children, many of whom instigated the men to further work of blood.

The rioters then burned the provost-marshal's building to the ground, but their malice had only begun. Among the most inhuman acts of the riots were those directed not at the draft offices or the Union army but at blacks. And, the *Times* reporter tells us, the mob mentality had now spread to the women and children in the crowd:

The Orphan Asylum for Colored Children was visited by the mob about 4 o'clock. . . . Hundreds, and perhaps thousands of the rioters, the majority of whom were women and children, entered the premises, and in the most excited and violent manner they ransacked and plundered the building from cellar to garret. The building was located in the most pleasant and healthy portion of the City. It was purely a charitable institution. In it there are on an average 600 or 800 homeless colored orphans. . . .

After the entire building had been ransacked, and every article deemed worth carrying away had been taken—and this included even the little garments for the orphans, which were contributed by the benevolent ladies of this City—the premises were fired on the first floor . . . , and after an hour and a half of labor on the part of the mob, it was in flames in all

parts. . . . There is now scarcely one brick left upon another of the Orphan Asylum.

The *Times* article reports that at least a dozen black people were beaten to death that day, many in the manner of the following account:

Among the most diabolical of these outrages . . . is that of a negro cart man living in Carmine Street [in the Greenwich Village section of New York]. About 8 o'clock in the evening as he was coming out of the stable, after having put up his horses, he was attacked by a crowd of about 400 men and boys, who beat him with clubs and paving stones till he was

An Englishman's View of Race Relations in the North

In 1862 English journalist Edward Dicey visited the United States and wrote extensively about the conditions of African Americans in the North. What he observed was a rigidly segregated society, as we see in this excerpt taken from Smith and Judah's Life in the North During the Civil War.

"Everywhere and at all seasons the coloured people form a separate community. In the public streets you hardly ever see a coloured person in company with a white, except in the capacity of servant. Boston, indeed, is the only town I visited where I ever observed black men and women walking about frequently with white people. I never by any chance, in the Free States, saw a coloured man dining at a public table, or mixing socially in any manner with white men, or dressed as a man well to do in the world, or occupying any position, however

humble, in which he was placed in authority over white persons. On board the river steamboats, the commonest and homeliest of working men has a right to dine, and does dine, at the public meals; but, for coloured passengers, there is always a separate table. At the great hotels there is, as with us, a servant's table, but the coloured servants are not allowed to dine in common with the white. At the inns, in the barber's shops, on board the steamers, and in most hotels, the servants are more often than not coloured people. . . . White servants will not associate with black on terms of equality. . . . I hardly ever remember seeing a black employed as shopman, or placed in any post of responsibility. As a rule, the blacks you meet in the Free States are shabbily if not squalidly dressed; and, as far as I could learn, the instances of black men having money by trade in the North, are very few in number."

lifeless, and then hung him to a tree opposite the burying ground. Not being yet satisfied with their devilish work, they set fire to his clothes and danced and yelled and swore their horrid oaths around his burning corpse. The charred body of the poor victim was still hanging upon the tree at a late hour last evening.[71]

The Copperheads and Other Antiwar Politicians

Antiwar activities were not limited to New York and other Eastern cities, although opposition from the "Midwest"—Michigan, Indiana, Illinois, and Ohio—was usually more civil. Most of the political opposition to President Lincoln and the Republican Party came from the Democratic Party. Almost from the outset of the war, the Democratic Party was divided into two factions: the so-called War Democrats, led by former senator Stephen Douglas and General George McClellan; and the Peace Democrats, led by Senator Clement Vallandigham of Dayton, Ohio. War Democrats supported Lincoln's military objectives of defeating the Confederacy and preserving the Union, but they opposed certain Republican policies, including the emancipation of Southern slaves. Republicans and War Democrats alike looked with suspicion on the radical ideas of the Peace Democrats, whom they labeled "Copperheads," after the poisonous snake. The Peace Democrats, or Copperheads, denounced the entire war as a failure. Although they did not publicly support draft riots, the rhetoric of the Copperheads was strongly antigovernment and

A policeman protects a black family during the draft riots in this Civil War–era cartoon, entitled "Their Brave Protector." Northerners unleashed their fury against blacks, whom they blamed for the draft and their economic hardships.

Former slaves flocked to the North in unprecedented numbers during the Civil War years, taking shelter with other refugees in segregated neighborhoods.

antiblack. They demanded a negotiated peace that granted all new territories and states the right to legalize slavery.

The Long Road to Equality

The Copperhead movement reached its peak in the fall of 1862, when the war effort looked rather grim. Several Copperheads ran for Congress and unseated their Republican opponents. By the end of 1863, however, the Emancipation Proclamation, the Conscription Act, and the use of black soldiers had all helped to seal the South's fate. Then the unrest in Northern cities began to calm, and

the Copperhead movement faded away. The opposition to equal rights for blacks, however, remained strong.

By the end of the war, the number of blacks living in the North had climbed from a little over two hundred thousand to over one million. Although most worked in unskilled jobs, a growing number attended public schools and became lawyers, doctors, ministers, and shopkeepers. For the most part, however, the cities remained segregated, with black communities, which supported their own churches, newspapers, shops, and civic organizations, isolated from white society.

Middle- and upper-class African Americans formed local, regional, and national

Northerners congregate during an abolitionist meeting. Enlightened Northerners criticized the injustice of segregation and worked to extend civil rights to all Americans, regardless of race.

organizations to assist impoverished former slaves, who often arrived in towns and cities with no possessions except the clothes they wore. One former slave, Elizabeth Keckley, became a successful dressmaker in Washington, D.C., and a friend of Mary Todd Lincoln's. Keckley organized the Freedmen and Soldiers' Relief Association, which staged parades and gala fund-raising balls. The association used the money to open schools, medical clinics, and cafeterias in the black communities and to provide other assistance for former slaves and black veterans.

Despite their efforts to integrate within Northern society, most black Americans lived in a world of legal restrictions and social segregation. They had obtained freedom from slavery, but they had hardly gained the rights of citizens. Before 1870, only five New England states allowed blacks to vote, and in New York, black voters had to pay a poll tax that was not required of white voters; the amount—$250—was about a full year's wages for an unskilled laborer. Inte-

grated schools were also extremely rare outside New England. In most Northern states, hospitals, schools, prisons, and even churches remained segregated.

A portion of the Northern white population recognized the unfairness of segregation. Susan B. Anthony, the famous abolitionist and women's rights leader, noted the irony of fighting a war to free slaves from physical bondage but then keeping them in economic and political shackles: "While the cruel slave driver lacerates the black man's mortal body, we, of the North, flay the spirit."[72] A senator from Massachusetts, Charles Sumner, began a crusade to outlaw segregation. Soon Congress had banned slavery in all U.S. territories, removed federal restrictions against black postal workers, allowed blacks to testify in federal courts, and integrated the congressional galleries.

Changes came more slowly at the state and local levels, but pressure for racial equality grew. Protesters rallied outside segregated schools, hospitals, and theaters. In the most progressive churches, abolitionists managed to desegregate church pews, so that blacks and whites sat together. Some of these churches also invited black ministers to preach to their mixed congregations.

Like so many other facets of life in the North during the Civil War, race relations were a confusing mix of forward steps and retreats. The end of slavery and the northward migration of former slaves brought a significant minority population to the North for the first time. The mixture of blacks, European immigrants, descendants of the original American colonists, and Native Americans yielded a rich blend of cultures. At the same time, many Northerners viewed these changes as a threat to their way of life. In this way, too, the Civil War era ushered in many of the racial and political tensions that typify American life today.

A Catalyst for Change

Any major war is bound to have lasting effects on the nations involved, but it is safe to say that no major war has so profoundly changed American society as did the Civil War. First, it is the only major war fought on American soil since the nation was founded. It exacted a heavier toll in American lives than all other wars in which the United States participated, combined.

War and the Economy

This war, like most, stimulated the economy. The Civil War, however, not only provided a temporary stimulus; it sped up permanent changes that touched virtually every aspect of American business, industry, and agriculture. The demand for food and farm labor resulted in the introduction of new machinery and technology to American farmers. It also brought a large number of American women into the labor force for the first time. In Northern cities, the war helped spur the technological revolution of mass production. Although many of these innovations appeared first in munitions plants, they were carried over to peacetime manufacturing as well.

The unique crises and political developments related to the Civil War also permanently increased the federal government's involvement in the economy. The Legal Tender Act of 1861 created the American monetary system that we take for granted today.

This, like so many legislative actions of the Civil War period, probably would not have occurred if the secession of eleven Southern states had not altered the composition of the U.S. Congress. For example, the Republican-controlled Congress enacted the first federal income tax, to help support the war effort. More significantly, since its inception, the Republican Party had led the movement for a stronger federal government, with the power to support interstate commerce and public education. Republicans had proposed numerous federal actions to help develop agriculture and trade in the West; but as long as powerful Southern advocates of states' rights remained in Congress, these measures were doomed.

When Southern senators and representatives withdrew, following the secession of their respective states, however, Republicans enacted a sweeping legislative program that included the Homestead Act, laws establishing financing for land grant colleges and universities, and laws providing land and loans for the building of a transcontinental railroad, which was completed in 1869. Most of this legislation, of course, benefited the Northern states, which is but one example of how the Civil War helped the North economically while driving the South into ruin.

Consequently, the South would take decades to recover from the devastation of the Civil War. The war hit the South much harder than the North for several reasons. First, quite obviously, the South lost the war, having expended almost all its wealth and resources in the process. Second, the war was fought almost entirely on Southern soil, and so hundreds of towns and even a few major cities, like Atlanta and Richmond, were demolished. Thus, instead of the economic miracle experienced by the North, the South experienced almost total economic collapse. Furthermore, Southern agriculture was geared toward cash crops—tobacco and cotton—rather than subsistence crops, like grains and other food products.

Still, the South might have recovered much more quickly after the war if the federal government had provided the same kind of economic support it directed to states in the North and the West. Instead, the South was treated punitively during the years immediately following the Civil War, known as the Reconstruction Era. Before the Civil War, many Americans in the North and the South had important ties, either through business or family. After the war, most business ties were broken, and consequently, fewer family ties were made. While the Northern states were now linked by transcontinental railroads and thousands of miles of canals, the South remained isolated, in the economic backwaters of the nation.

Finally, the Civil War sparked smoldering ethnic and racial tensions in Northern society. Some European immigrants had experienced the frustration of unrealized dreams and unfulfilled ambitions before the war, but

The Civil War brought tremendous changes to America. One of the most notable changes in society occurred when droves of women entered the workforce for the first time in the nation's history.

as the number of immigrants swelled and the gap between the rich and the poor expanded, those frustrations intensified. With the draft issue as the spark, the Civil War was enough to set the smoldering tinder of frustration ablaze. Most of that frustration was channeled toward black Americans, newly arrived in Northern cities.

An End to Slavery

Unquestionably, the greatest good to come from the Civil War was the end of slavery. Unfortunately, the man most responsible for making that happen, Abraham Lincoln, was assassinated by a fanatical Southern sympathizer just five days after Robert E. Lee surrendered to Ulysses S. Grant at Appomattox Courthouse, Virginia, ending the Civil War. Whether Lincoln would or could have done any more than his successors to assure former slaves a smoother transition to liberty will nev-

er be known, but the federal government was extremely slow to assist the black population through this difficult time. With no experience in seeking jobs or providing for themselves, many former slaves found life to be nearly as difficult as in their days of slavery.

The Fifteenth Amendment to the Constitution, ratified in 1870, explicitly prohibits the federal government, or any state, from denying the right to vote to U.S. citizens "on account of race, color, or previous condition of servitude." Although that is the law, it took three-quarters of a century for the federal government to strictly enforce it and to support such logical extensions as the right to hold public office. Meanwhile, the relationship between blacks and whites was often marred by irrational fears and biases. To vote in most states, black citizens had to pass literacy tests or pay poll taxes that were not required of white citizens. In most cities, black families were actively discouraged from living in white neighborhoods, and black chil-

The once thriving city of Richmond, Virginia, was devastated by the war, as this 1865 photograph attests.

Life in the North During the Civil War

Although freed from slavery, blacks in the North and the South continued to be treated as second-class citizens. Only within the past fifty years have blacks been able to achieve the same civil liberties granted to whites.

dren were not allowed to attend the same public schools as white children. When black people organized to defend their rights, the reaction of whites, fanned by the irrational fears of the unknown and the inflammatory rhetoric of white supremacy groups, was often violent.

Civil Rights

Gradually, through the education of all Americans and the influence of thousands of civic and religious leaders, both white and black, the federal government began to protect the civil rights of black citizens. While this country's schools, workplaces, and neighborhoods have become more integrated in the past fifty years, much of the racial tension of the past still lingers. The dreams of leaders like Martin Luther King Jr., that someday all people will be judged by their character and not by the color of their skin, have not yet been realized, but perhaps with increased knowledge of the lives of Americans during the influential years of the Civil War, we will understand the roots of racial tension and be better able to put the past behind us.

Notes

Introduction: Civil War: A Tragic Chapter in American Life

1. George Templeton Strong, *Diary: The Civil War, 1860–1865.* Edited by Allan Nevins and Milton Halsey Thomas. New York: Macmillan, 1962.

Chapter 1: The Wheels of Change

2. James M. McPherson, *Battle Cry of Freedom: The Civil War Era.* New York: Oxford University Press, 1988.
3. Quoted in Phillip Shaw Paludan, *"A People's Contest": The Union and Civil War.* New York: Harper & Row, 1988.
4. Quoted in McPherson, *Battle Cry of Freedom.*
5. Quoted in McPherson, *Battle Cry of Freedom.*
6. Quoted in McPherson, *Battle Cry of Freedom.*
7. Quoted in Paludan, *"A People's Contest."*
8. Quoted in Paludan, *"A People's Contest."*
9. Quoted in McPherson, *Battle Cry of Freedom.*
10. Quoted in McPherson, *Battle Cry of Freedom.*
11. Quoted in Timothy Levi Biel, *America's Wars: The Civil War.* San Diego: Lucent Books, 1991.
12. Quoted in Paludan, *"A People's Contest."*
13. Quoted in Paludan, *"A People's Contest."*
14. Quoted in McPherson, *Battle Cry of Freedom.*
15. Quoted in Paludan, *"A People's Contest."*
16. Quoted in Paludan, *"A People's Contest."*
17. Harriet Beecher Stowe, *Uncle Tom's Cabin*, 1852. Reprinted, New York: Modern Library, 1985.
18. Quoted in Paludan, *"A People's Contest."*

Chapter 2: A Call to Arms

19. Quoted in Paludan, *"A People's Contest."*
20. Quoted in Paludan, *"A People's Contest."*
21. Quoted in Paludan, *"A People's Contest."*
22. Quoted in James M. McPherson, *Ordeal by Fire: The Civil War and Reconstruction.* New York: Knopf, 1982.
23. Quoted in Paludan, *"A People's Contest."*
24. Quoted in McPherson, *Battle Cry of Freedom.*
25. Quoted in McPherson, *Battle Cry of Freedom.*
26. Quoted in McPherson, *Battle Cry of Freedom.*
27. Quoted in McPherson, *Battle Cry of Freedom.*
28. Quoted in Cecil Perkins, *Northern Editorials on Secession.* New York: Simon & Schuster, 1942.
29. Quoted in Paludan, *"A People's Contest."*
30. Allen C. Guelzo, *The Crisis of the American Republic: A History of the Civil War and Reconstruction Era.* New York: St. Martin's Press, 1995.
31. Quoted in James I. Robertson, *The Civil War: Tenting Tonight, The Soldier's Life.* Alexandria, VA: Time-Life Books, 1984.
32. Quoted in Robertson, *The Civil War: Tenting Tonight.*

Chapter 3: Life in a Union Army Camp

33. Quoted in Robertson, *The Civil War: Tenting Tonight.*

34. Quoted in Robertson, *The Civil War: Tenting Tonight*.

35. Quoted in Robertson, *The Civil War: Tenting Tonight*.

36. Quoted in Robertson, *The Civil War: Tenting Tonight*.

37. Quoted in Robertson, *The Civil War: Tenting Tonight*.

38. Quoted in Robertson, *The Civil War: Tenting Tonight*.

39. Quoted in Robertson, *The Civil War: Tenting Tonight*.

40. Quoted in Robertson, *The Civil War: Tenting Tonight*.

41. Quoted in Robertson, *The Civil War: Tenting Tonight*.

42. Quoted in Robertson, *The Civil War: Tenting Tonight*.

43. Quoted in McPherson, *Battle Cry of Freedom*.

44. Quoted in J. Matthew Gallman, *The North Fights the Civil War: The Home Front*. Chicago: Ivan R. Dee, 1994.

45. Quoted in Gallman, *The North Fights the Civil War*.

Chapter 4: The War's Economic Impact

46. Quoted in Donald Dale Jackson, *The Civil War: Twenty Million Yankees, The Northern Home Front*. New York: Time-Life Books, 1985.

47. Quoted in Jackson, *The Civil War: Twenty Million Yankees*.

48. Quoted in Jackson, *The Civil War: Twenty Million Yankees*.

49. Quoted in Jackson, *The Civil War: Twenty Million Yankees*.

50. Quoted in George Winston Smith and Charles Judah, *Life in the North During the Civil War*. Albuquerque: University of New Mexico Press, 1966.

51. Quoted in Jackson, *The Civil War: Twenty Million Yankees*.

52. Quoted in Smith and Judah, *Life in the North During the Civil War*.

53. Quoted in Smith and Judah, *Life in the North During the Civil War*.

54. Quoted in Jackson, *The Civil War: Twenty Million Yankees*.

55. Quoted in Smith and Judah, *Life in the North During the Civil War*.

56. Quoted in Smith and Judah, *Life in the North During the Civil War*.

57. Quoted in Jackson, *The Civil War: Twenty Million Yankees*.

Chapter 5: Life in the Rural North

58. Quoted in Daniel E. Sutherland, *The Expansion of Everyday Life, 1860–1876*. New York: Harper & Row, 1989.

59. Quoted in Sutherland, *The Expansion of Everyday Life*.

60. Quoted in Sutherland, *The Expansion of Everyday Life*.

Chapter 6: Life in the Northern City

61. Quoted in Carole Rifkind, *A Field Guide to American Architecture*. New York: Bonanza Books, 1980.

62. Quoted in Sutherland, *The Expansion of Everyday Life*.

63. Quoted in Sutherland, *The Expansion of Everyday Life*.

64. Quoted in Sutherland, *The Expansion of Everyday Life*.

65. Quoted in Sutherland, *The Expansion of Everyday Life*.

66. Quoted in Sutherland, *The Expansion of Everyday Life*.

67. Quoted in Sutherland, *The Expansion of Everyday Life*.

Chapter 7: Racial and Political Tensions

68. Quoted in Gallman, *The North Fights the Civil War*.

69. Quoted in Gallman, *The North Fights the Civil War*.

70. Quoted in Gallman, *The North Fights the Civil War*.

71. Quoted in Gallman, *The North Fights the Civil War*.

72. Quoted in Gallman, *The North Fights the Civil War*.

For Further Reading

Ronald H. Bailey et al., *Brother Against Brother: Time-Life Books History of the Civil War*. New York: Prentice Hall, 1990. A remarkable introduction to the Civil War and the regional tensions that caused it. This book contains a treasury of photographs, maps, and illustrations to guide novices and hold their interest throughout.

Timothy Levi Biel, *America's Wars: The Civil War*. San Diego: Lucent Books, 1991. A clear, concise history of the causes, major campaigns, and effects of the Civil War. A rich source of eyewitness accounts and interesting historical, biographical sidebars.

David Donald, *Divided We Fought*. New York: Macmillan, 1961. A comprehensive illustrated history of the Civil War written for the young adult.

Donald Dale Jackson, *The Civil War: Twenty Million Yankees, The Northern Home Front*. New York: Time-Life Books, 1985. A well-researched social critique for the history novice, this book features a number of eyewitness accounts and a feast of photographs.

Milton Meltzer, ed., *Voices from the Civil War: A Documentary History of the Great American Conflict*. New York: HarperCollins, 1989. A good introduction to source histories of the Civil War, this collection of excerpts from letters and diaries of soldiers is intriguing without being overwhelming.

Colin T. Naylor, *Civil War Days in a Country Village*. Peekskill, NY: Highland Press, 1961. This book focuses on the domestic and community life of one small New England town during the Civil War. Good selection of photographs.

James I. Robertson, *The Civil War: Tenting Tonight, The Soldier's Life*. Alexandria, VA: Time-Life Books, 1984. Another in the Time-Life *Civil War Series*, this book brings to life the experience of the Union soldier behind the lines. Excellent and abundant photographs.

Geoffrey C. Ward, *The Civil War: An Illustrated History*. New York: Knopf, 1990. Though the text may be too dense for a young audience, the photographs and maps are outstanding.

Additional Works Consulted

Everett Dick, *The Sod-House Frontier*. Lincoln, NE: Johnsen Publishing Company, 1954. An extraordinarily thorough account of the settling of the northern plains.

Michael P. Dineen et al., *America's Historic Houses*. Waukesha, WI: Country Beautiful, 1967. Descriptions and photographs of one hundred of America's most famous historical homes.

Carl Russell Fisk, *The Rise of the Common Man, 1830–1850*. New York: Macmillan, 1927. One of the earliest social histories of everyday life in the mid–nineteenth century.

J. Matthew Gallman, *The North Fights the Civil War: The Home Front*. Chicago: Ivan R. Dee, 1994. One of several recently published social histories of the Northern home front, this book includes an exceptional chapter on racial tensions in the period.

Wendell Phillips Garrison and Francis Jackson Garrison, *William Lloyd Garrison, 1805–1887: The Story of His Life Told by His Children*. New York: Century Company, 1889. An extremely flattering biography of the founder of the abolitionist movement.

Paul W. Gates, *Agriculture and the Civil War*. New York: Knopf, 1965. Examines agriculture in both North and South and explains thoroughly how the Civil War affected every aspect of farming, from crop selection and harvesting to raising livestock, using new machinery, and labor practices.

Allen C. Guelzo, *The Crisis of the American Republic: A History of the Civil War and Reconstruction Era*. New York: St. Martin's Press, 1995. A superior example of several recent social histories of the Civil War and Reconstruction period. Thorough scholarship and documentation support intriguing insights.

X. J. Kennedy, ed., *Literature: An Introduction to Poetry, Prose, and Drama*. New York: HarperCollins, 1995. An anthology of literature from around the world.

James M. McPherson, *Battle Cry of Freedom: The Civil War Era*. New York: Oxford University Press, 1988. The Pulitzer Prize–winning social history places a strong emphasis on the political context in which the events of this period occur.

———, *Ordeal by Fire: The Civil War and Reconstruction*. New York: Knopf, 1982. Recognized by Civil War scholars as an authoritative history, this work combines meticulous scholarship with an engaging style and an interesting approach.

Phillip Shaw Paludan, *"A People's Contest": The Union and Civil War*. New York: Harper & Row, 1988. An extremely well researched social history that covers the political, economic, social, and domestic effects of the Civil War conflict. Superb scholarship, but visual aids are negligible.

Cecil Perkins, *Northern Editorials on Secession*. New York: Simon & Schuster, 1942. An excellent collection of primary sources presenting a wide spectrum of opinion on this very specific topic.

Carole Rifkind, *A Field Guide to American Architecture*. New York: Bonanza Books, 1980. Abundant photographs and drawings support a fascinating history of American architecture.

George Winston Smith and Charles Judah, *Life in the North During the Civil War*. Albuquerque: University of New Mexico Press, 1966. A source history of the North during the Civil War era; draws from an exhaustive range of newspapers, magazines, diaries, speeches, and monographs.

George Templeton Strong, *Diary: The Civil War, 1860–1865*. Edited by Allan Nevins and Milton Halsey Thomas. New York: Macmillan, 1962. Among the most often-quoted diaries of the Civil War era, this book shows the outlook and concerns of an upper-class New Yorker who observes the events of the Civil War period from the home front.

Daniel E. Sutherland, *The Expansion of Everyday Life, 1860–1876*. New York: Harper & Row, 1989. Part of the Everyday Life in America Series, this book contains clear, vivid descriptions of home, work, and community in the Civil War and Reconstruction era, without being concerned with the Civil War itself. Its selection of photographs gives a strong visual sense of what it must have been like to live during this period of American history.

Agatha Young, *The Women and the Crisis*. New York: McDowell, Obolensky, 1959. An outstanding treatment of the women of the North during the Civil War era; their experiences and activities deserve a place in history.

Index

Yankee ingenuity and,
56–59
inflation, 100, 101–102
inventions, 56
printing press, 20
reaper, 52
sewing machine, 19, 56
steamboat, 14
telegraph, 20
Ives, James M., 67

Judah, Charles, 16, 28, 46,
61, 87, 100, 105

Keckley, Elizabeth, 108
King, Curtis, 36
King, Martin Luther, 113

laborers. *See* working class
labor unions. *See* unions
Lee, Robert E., 83, 112
Legal Tender Act, 51, 110
Levi Strauss Company, 70
*Life in the North During the
Civil War* (Smith and
Judah), 16, 28, 46, 61, 87,
100, 105
Lincoln, Abraham, 12, 83,
112
black soldiers and, 46, 48
Conscription Act and,
43–44
emancipation controversy
and, 99–100
homesteading and, 74–75
plans for war, 27, 44
on secession, 9, 27, 99–
100
slavery issue and, 8–9, 26,
27, 99–100
Lincoln, Mary Todd, 108
Lincoln, Tad, 31
literacy rates, 20, 21
*Literature: An Introduction
to Poetry, Prose, and Drama* (Kennedy), 15

log houses, 77
machinery
in farming industry, 52–53,
69
in oil industry, 55
magazines, 39, 53, 88, 89
Mann, Horace, 20
manufacturing industry
criticism of products and,
60, 62
in economic crisis, 50
expansion of, 14, 18, 54, 56
tenement system and, 94
Mayflower Society, 81
McClellan, George, 106
McCormick, Cyrus, 52
McGuffey Reader, 21
McPherson, James, 14, 51
medical profession, 42, 45,
84–85
*Merchants Magazine and
Review*, 52
middle class, 81, 84
blacks in, 107–108
as consumers, 86–88
farm families as, 67–68, 72
housing of, 85–86
money, paper, 50, 57
as national currency, 51
monopolies, 59

National Association of Base
Ball Players, 90–91, 93
National League of Profes-
sional Baseball Clubs, 93
Native Americans, 55, 79, 89
newspapers
growth of, 20, 21, 88
reporters, in war, 39
New York Daily Sun, 62
New York Evening Post, 82
New York Herald, 10, 60, 62,
96
New York Times, 18, 103–106
New York Tribune, 10, 20,
25, 28, 50, 100

normal schools, 20
North Fights the Civil War
(Gallman), 46
Northerners, 16, 18, 23–24,
110–12
on black soldiers, 46, 48
emancipation and, 98,
100–102
financial crisis among,
49–50
profit from war, 53–59
on secession, 26–27
on slavery, 12, 25
Norton, Oliver, 38

"O Captain, My Captain"
(Whitman), 15
oil industry, 55

parks, 89
Peace Democrats, 106
Pendleton, George, 51
photography, 39
physicians, 42, 45, 84–85
pioneer families, 76–79
police departments, 83–84
poll tax, 108, 112
poor people. *See* working
class
population growth, 13,
80–81, 107
prejudice. *See* racism
printing press, 20
prizefighting, 89, 91
prostitution, 41, 45
Protestants, 20–21, 22, 101
public school systems. *See*
education
Puritanism, 20–21, 88–89

racism
black soldiers as targets of,
46, 47–48
draft riots and, 104–106
emancipation and, 98–99,
101–102

Picture Credits

About the Author

Timothy Levi Biel was born and raised in eastern Montana. A graduate of Rocky Mountain College, he received a Ph.D. in literary studies from Washington State University. He teaches English at Tarrant County Community College in Hurst, Texas.

He is the author of numerous nonfiction books, many of which are part of the highly acclaimed Zoobooks series for young readers, in addition to *Pompeii: World Disasters, The Age of Feudalism, The Crusades,* and several other books for Lucent Books.